W9-BXV-130

WHAT OTHERS ARE SAYING ABOUT THIS BOOK:

"Charlie Ware has written a book that takes a fresh look at truth principles, bringing to them a delightful and easy way to remember them and to apply them where it counts—in our everyday lives."
—REV. ALAN A. ROWBOTHAM, MINISTER

"This book spoke clearly to my issues of procrastination and typically taking on too much. Charlie's gentle openness and willingness to share his many personal examples have helped in my growth process."
—ANNE S. FISHKIN, PH.D., CO-AUTHOR OF
INVESTIGATING CREATIVITY IN YOUTH: RESEARCH AND METHODS

"It re-inspired me to keep plugging forward on my journey toward goodness in life and in re-connecting with the god-self within me."
—DAVID KESSLER, AUTHOR OF *LOVE & BEYOND:
YOUR JOURNEY ON EARTH WITH GOD*

"Reading this remarkable book provided me with many deeply emotional, liberating experiences."
—DEBRA BUCKHANNON, BRAIN CANCER SURVIVOR

"Thanks Charlie for reminding me that each of us is the person we'd like to become. A wonderful 'wayfinding' tool for life's journey."
—DIANE MACKNIGHT, PRESIDENT, MACKNIGHT ASSOCIATES

"When life seems overwhelming, read Chapter 8. It changed my life!"
—F. WILLIAM KROESSER, PH.D., UNIVERSITY PROFESSOR (RET.)

"When I got this book I was feeling overwhelmed most of the time. Now I am much more at peace with myself, my children, my wife, co-workers, and those that I meet as I go through my day-to-day life."
—FRED BELL, QUALITY TRAINING SPECIALIST

"This book has changed my thinking. It is inspiring, full of wisdom and practical tips for handling the challenges of life."
—GARRY MILLER, COMPUTER SYSTEMS ANALYST

"I loved learning how to be in this world differently."
—HELEN DOUGLASS, HOMEMAKER

"The real life examples show how to make real life application. This book has been a godsend."
—K. JANE FRIEND, RADIO PERSONALITY

"This book contains deceptively simple antidotes to Murphy's Law. I'm reminded there is a different way to 'be' that is empowering, loving, and fun."
—JUDITH SULT, MARKETING CONSULTANT

"I feel very honest, refreshed, and relaxed from reading this book. I find myself smiling more and stressing less. What a great feeling!"
—LINDSAY WINSLOW, ELEMENTARY SCHOOL TEACHER

"This book captures Charlie's humor, love, and inextinguishable joy."
—MARCY TRIANOSKY, COLLEGE WRITING INSTRUCTOR

"A hands-on guide for learning to Trust."
—PATTI RONDOLINO, PRESIDENT, PHOENIX RISING PROMOTIONS, INC.

"I love the beauty and simplicity of this book. I came away from it with a relaxed sigh, a soft smile, and a sense of relief. The Universe knows what it's doing."
—SHARON JEBENS, BOOK STORE MANAGER

"This book not only helped me identify areas that may need my attention, but also gave me gentle, sound guidance on walking the talk of a truly spiritual being."
—SHERRY STIVER, BOOKSTORE/GIFT SHOP OWNER

"After reading and working through 'Charlie's Laws' I have a more trusting relationship with my God and have become a better servant because of it. My life has a new direction."
—TORI CHARLES, DENTAL ASSISTANT

Murphy's Law
Repealed!

Murphy's Law Repealed!

everything turns out right . . . when you let it

Charles H. Ware, Ph.D.

FIRST EDITION

CHARLIE'S LAW, INC. ❦ SAFETY HARBOR, FLORIDA

Murphy's Law Repealed!
Everything Turns Out Right . . . When You Let It
By Charles H. Ware, Ph.D.

Published by:
Charlie's Law, Inc.
853 Main Street, Suite B
Safety Harbor, Florida 34695
(727) 723-1070

All rights reserved. No part of this book may be reproduced or transmitted in any form or by any means, electronic or mechanical, including photocopying, recording or by any information storage and retrieval system, without written permission from the author, except for inclusion of brief quotations in a review.

Copyright © 2004 Charles H. Ware, Ph.D.
First Edition
Printed in the United States of America

Publisher's Cataloging-in-Publication
(Provided by Quality Books, Inc.)

    Ware, Charles H.
        Murphy's law repealed! : everything turns out right--
    when you let it / Charles H. Ware. -- 1st ed.
        p. cm.
        Includes bibliographical references and index.
        LCCN 2003112880
        ISBN 0-9743505-0-8

        1. Spirituality. 2. Success. 3. Conduct of life.
    4. Inspiration. I. Title.

    BL624.W37 2004   158.1
                         QBI03-700648

To Sharon
my loving supporter

to Fred
my best friend

and to Lyn
my constant guide in writing this book

Acknowledgements

(in order of appearance)

Ellen and *Laura*, for helping me be a more loving father.

Haggott Beckhart, for demonstrating again and again the power of gentility.

Fred Schwettmann, for pointing me towards many books, sharing many ideas with me, and challenging my ideas.

Trudie Evangelou, for introducing me to the mind/body relationship.

June Mehta, for relating to me more lovingly than anyone ever had before, introducing me to the writings of J. Krishnamurti, and giving me some concepts I have used over and over again and now appear in this book.

Martha and *Wayne Corley, Bob Terry*, and *Eva Jo* and *Frank Wu*, for talking me into taking the EST training (now The Forum) and providing a support group to work out some of my ideas.

My wife, *Sharon Mayes*, for loving me more than anyone else has, for teaching me to let go of my negative humor, to be kinder, gentler, and more loving, for supporting my growth and change, for introducing me to *A Course in Miracles*, and for teaching me to dance.

Michael Toms and all of the staff at *New Dimensions Radio*, for introducing me to the ideas of more wonderful people than I can count . . . ideas from a wide variety of spiritual paths, cultures, and disciplines.

Jerry Jampolsky, for teaching me that *Love Is Letting Go of Fear*, thereby helping me let go of fear.

The volunteer staff at many *Southeastern Unitarian Universalist Summer Institutes (SUUSIs)* allowing me to conduct workshops in conflict resolution, *A Course in Miracles*, creativity, and *Charlie's Law*™, enabling me to clarify my ideas and have them tested.

The Voice in *A Course in Miracles,* for teaching me most of what I have learned about forgiveness, practicing forgiveness, letting go of fear, and becoming a loving person.

Dolores Smith's guest, for seeing my spirit guide and introducing me to him, thus letting me know I am not alone.

Kathryn Rhoads, for sharing her keen perception of beauty in nature and people, as well as her questions and wonderments, which helped me discover what I believe.

John Langdon, for stimulating me to create *Charlie's Law*™ and its posters, as well as encouraging me to publish them.

Nancy Louise Mottesheard, for helping me to realize that my life can be more spiritual, more prayerful, and more loving.

Holly Forester-Miller, for demonstrating the strength of the mind/body connection.

Amy Buckingham, for her creative expression of *Charlie's Law*™ principles.

The people who have given me permission to share their stories with you, thereby enriching this book.

Lyn Rainbow, for raising my level of spiritual awareness, strengthening my bond with Holy Spirit, and guiding me as I wrote this book.

Holy Spirit, for waking me up and helping me on innumerable occasions, for enabling me to allow good things to happen, for giving me faith that everything was in Divine Order even when things happened that I didn't like or understand, and for bringing to me the people and events that have nurtured me.

Alexandra MacKnight, for her loving support and editorial assistance.

Rev. Alan Rowbotham, for teaching and exemplifying many of the principles of this book

Countless other people—*friends, relatives,* and *strangers*—for teaching me love by extending their love and for teaching me to love through their calls for love.

To all of these people and to many more with whom I have related at work, at church, while traveling, and in everyday life, I give my heartfelt thanks for helping me to live with more peace, love, and joy.

TABLE OF CONTENTS

PREFACE

Prior to my retirement from the business world, I often saw my employees' work areas adorned with posters proudly proclaiming Murphy's Law: *Anything that can go wrong, will!*

This negative view of the universe apparently started as a whimsical saying, and achieved cult-like status, embedding itself in the consciousness and subconscious of people who use it to describe their lives and their expectations. Murphy's Law not only appears on posters, it is often verbalized to explain disappointing results of all kinds, and to make dire predictions.

Charlie Ware has had the courage and commitment to defy Murphy's Law. While traveling across Texas with a friend, Charlie told his companion that he did not appreciate the frequent references to Murphy's Law as an excuse for setbacks and failures. When his friend challenged him to come up with something better, Charlie rose to the occasion and Charlie's Law was born: *Everything turns out right . . . when you let it.*

Charlie did not invent this idea. It is a universal principle, which he likens to the theory of gravity. Newton didn't invent gravity, he simply explained and described it. So it is with Charlie's Law. *Everything turns out right . . . when you let it* is the way the universe operates naturally, and the way we can realize increased peace and joy. In this book, Charlie explains how to use Charlie's Law to enrich our daily lives.

If you find yourself thinking in terms of Murphy's Law to explain why things happen to you and you desire a life free of anxiety, this book is for you.

If you have already moved beyond Murphy's Law to a more positive view of the universe, *Murphy's Law Repealed!* will help solidify that view and help you expand it in new, creative ways. Although the task of understanding and internalizing the principle that *Everything turns out right . . . when you let it* requires thought and effort, Charlie's techniques are easy. Throughout the book, he guides you with examples typical of everyday experiences, revealing the simple secret of bringing joy and love into your life.

The proof of Charlie's Law is in the role models it creates. I have known Charlie Ware for over forty years. When I first met him he was an expert in industrial research and development. As a new college graduate, I often sought his advice on technical issues and he was always willing to spare the time to help me out. As I interacted more and more with Charlie, I discovered not only a brilliant person with a keen analytical mind, but a man who radiated a kind of love and caring that I rarely see in others. To me he is the role model for *Everything turns out right . . . when you let it.*

I have said many times, "When I grow up, I want to be like Charlie." I can think of no better way to achieve that goal than by careful study and application of the principles in this wonderful book.

Fred Schwettmann, Ph.D.
Retired

President and COO Read-Rite Corp. (1992-1997)
VP Hewlett Packard Co. (1986-1992)

INTRODUCTION

Murphy's Law Repealed!

The traditional form of Murphy's Law is: *Anything that can go wrong, will.* For more than fifty years, it has been creeping into the American psyche unchallenged. It is a catch-phrase used to predict lapses and failures, as well as to rationalize past errors and mishaps.

Murphy's Law is a filter through which many people see their world, negatively and fearfully. It has been used to express anxiety, fear, and victimhood. Most importantly, it has kept us from seeing that the world is a safe place in which we can learn and grow.

For many people, Murphy's Law is an assumption about how the world works. It is a false assumption. In fact, we can safely assume that *everything turns out right, when you let it.* For the past fifteen years, I have witnessed countless examples of this principle in action. In writing this book, my objective has been to help you see the truth of it.

In the spring of 1994, my wife and I bought a house in Clearwater, Florida. As we were getting ready for our August move, I often had the feeling that I was going home. The feeling wasn't that I was going back to the Tampa Bay area where I had made my home for three years in the early 1980s, but that I was going home. I didn't understand my feelings.

A few months later while on a plane, I made notes in my journal, putting the day's date on every page. There were many notes and I wrote the date many times: July 12. It seemed vaguely familiar, and I wondered what that date meant to me. Was it someone's birthday? I couldn't think of anyone. I wrote the date a few more times. Then it came to me: July 12 was the day, exactly 20 years before, when I resigned from Texaco, my employer for 15 years.

On the plane that day, I realized I had been on a twenty-year journey and was now going home to myself.

Since that day, I have continued my inner journey to increase my understanding of how the world works, how misconceptions and misperceptions block my awareness of how the world works, and how to function more peacefully, lovingly, and joyfully. I have written this book to help you find your own joyful new sense of self by using your experiences to let go of fear, failure, judgment and conflict. I want to help you on your journey home to your true self.

The book centers on familiar situations, demonstrating how to transform anxious responses into peaceful, loving ones. Your perceptions will be guided away from fear of failure, from feelings of being overwhelmed, of being at the end of your rope, of being out of time, and of being less than, as well as feelings of lack of love, money, and "stuff." By owning those feelings, experiencing them differently, and letting go, you will find your way to a new sense of self.

How would your life be if you knew that everything turns out right? Would you live joyfully, with peace and love? I think so.

The purpose of this book is to enable you to recognize that, in truth, *everything **does** turn out right . . . when you let it.* The principle is a sweeping affirmation, grounded in reality. It applies to how you think about yourself and others. It applies to your relationships with yourself, your spouse or significant other, your children, relatives, friends, all the people at work, everyone. It applies to your relationships with your job, money and possessions. It applies to how you live and, perhaps most of all, to your relationship with your spiritual nature, which is part of you. This book will show you how to make the transition from where you are to living a life based upon this principle and to living more harmoniously.

How about everyone else? Can everything turn out right for them, too? The book shows that the answer is: "Yes, when they let it." And you can help them by demonstrating this principle.

This book will help you use your essential spiritual nature to be in the world differently, and to know it is a safe place. This is not wishful thinking. The book demonstrates repeatedly in a variety of everyday situations that *everything turns out right . . . when you let it.* I expect you will start out wishing it were true and end up knowing it is true.

Everything turns out right . . . is not the same as getting everything we want. Part of the principle is that we don't know what is right for us in any particular situation. When we think we do, we are likely to push for that outcome, which gets in the way of letting it turn out right. If we just let it, we'll recognize the "right" outcome when we see it.

My graduate education in engineering helped me enormously in gathering material for this book, long before knowing I was going to write it. I learned to be a keen observer of not just technical things but also of my outer experiences: life, myself, loved ones, and friends. Twenty years ago when my life was not working, I wanted to have more harmonious relationships with myself and with others. My inner guidance became a major force in my life and, together with my outer experience, taught me how to live with more love, peace, and joy.

The path I followed is simply my path. However, the way I found it is available to everyone: by listening to my inner guidance and following its direction to a new world. This book contains highlights of what I've learned while succeeding in living more and more harmoniously. Some of them are:

◇ There is enough of everything: things, loving relationships, and time, as well as opportunities for spiritual, personal, and professional growth.

◇ We are either succeeding or learning. The popular view of "succeeding" is getting what we want. "Learning" means getting a more spiritual picture, seeing the world differently, and realizing we often don't need what we think we want.

◇ Every challenge is a learning opportunity.

◇ When I use the power of forgiveness, I am on the path to love.

◇ When I am feeling upset or stressed, I can find the source within myself.

◈ When I am at peace, I can find the source within myself.

◈ My inner guidance is my greatest source of wisdom. It is always available and works when I listen, regardless of what I understand or believe about it. It could be God, Holy Spirit, Jesus, Universal Mind, or some other source.

◈ When I look at what is, without judgment, without trying to figure it out, without trying to understand why people are doing what they're doing, without resistance, without interpretation, without adding anything, and without questioning, I am at peace.

◈ When I relate to a child with love and integrity, peace will come to me first, next to the child, and then to our relationship.

◈ When I relate to anyone with love and integrity, peace will come to me first, next to the other person, and then to our relationship.

◈ My biggest obstacle to completing any task is getting started.

◈ Life gives me endless opportunities to choose peace.

◈ My relationships provide me with endless opportunities to choose peace.

◈ When I really understand that *everything turns out right . . . when you let it*, it's easy to relax and let everything turn out right.

◈ I greatly benefit when I have no emotional attachment to the outcome of my endeavors.

◈ Waging peace means choosing, over and over again, to do the kind, loving, giving, helpful thing.

◈ The love cycle works: be a loving person, do loving things, and have loving relationships.

◈ Extending love is part of my growth process.

◈ We can safely assume that everyone is doing the best they can.

I have learned these truths, have continued to improve my practice of them, and have deepened my understanding of them. This book shows how you can come to see them clearly and experience them for yourself in your everyday life.

In **Chapter 1, Murphy's Law Repealed!,** we see that we often don't know what is right for us in any particular situation, so we don't have to push for our solution. Following our inner guidance plays a vital role in everything turning out right.

Chapter 2, If You Need Something, It Will Come to You, shows that we learn what we need by what we get, even if we don't want what we get.

Chapter 3, When Faced with A Difficult Task, Start, looks at why tasks are difficult and the power of *Start!* It invites us to welcome difficult tasks; they are our teachers.

Chapter 4, Just when You Think You've Run out of Time, You're Done, describes how running out of time, "failure," and being done, "success," are perceptions, that is, choices we make.

Chapter 5, If at First You Don't Succeed, Relax and You Will, turns " . . . try, try again" upside down, exposes its pessimism, and offers a positive alternative. Relaxing includes working diligently on the task at hand.

In **You Are the Person You'd Like to Become, Chapter 6** reminds us that we are whole, complete, and perfect; we need do nothing. It teaches the value of experiencing ourselves as the person we'd like to become.

Chapter 7, Everything You Do That Comes from Love, Works describes the love cycle: be loving, do loving things and have loving relationships, with each element reinforcing the other two. The love cycle always works because we are filled with love in the process.

Chapter 8 recommends that **When Life Seems Overwhelming, Do Less.** When we already feel overwhelmed, we can't do more; we need to do less and commit to doing even less.

Chapter 9, If You Reach the End of Your Rope, Let Go and Fly, suggests we look at what we're holding on to, open up to our inner guidance, and develop trust in the answers we receive.

With *When You Choose Peace, You Get Peace, Chapter 10* shows that peace is a choice and includes having no emotional investment in the outcome. All of our relationships provide excellent opportunities to choose peace.

Chapter 11, Live Each Day as if It Were Your First, shows that without encumbrances from the past or anxieties about the future, we live joyously and with heightened awareness.

In *Chapter 12, When You Let Go, You Feel Joy*, the book concludes with guidance for letting go of unwanted personal characteristics in order to feel joy. It shows that letting go of any such characteristic involves a different way of being. This chapter also shows the power of being authentic, forgiving, loving, co-operative, okay with ourselves, compassionate, and relaxed. It shows how each of these ways of being can lead us to let go of the characteristic or behavior we would like to release.

Throughout the book you will find many examples taken from my personal experiences and those of my friends, relatives, loved ones, and acquaintances. Six exercises are also included so you can engage the material directly.

This book shows a different way of being. It invites you to see that *everything turns out right . . . when you let it.* The book is your bridge from where you are now to living out of the principle because you know it is true.

Charlie
Safety Harbor, FL
September 2003

1

Murphy's Law Repealed!

"Genius is nothing but a greater aptitude for patience."
—Attributed to George Louis Leclerc de Buffon

A bout 15 years ago, I was riding around Texas with a friend and business associate. Two or three times he mentioned Murphy's Law. (The traditional version of Murphy's Law is "Anything that can go wrong, will." It and scores of corollaries have been used to express anxiety and fear for over 50 years, often with humorous overtones.) Although I had heard it many times before, it just struck me as wrong that day: too negative and not funny anymore. I told him I'd like him not to use that expression. He agreed and challenged me to come up with something better.

Soon the idea came to me: "Everything turns out right, if you let it." My wife, Sharon, suggested "when" would be more affirmative than "if." That was it. *Everything turns out right . . . when you let it.*

I thought I had made the principle up just to be clever, but actually it was grounded (and still is) in my own experience. An incident from ten years earlier illustrates this point.

WHAT'S RIGHT?

I was on a late-afternoon flight from St. Louis to Minneapolis, planning to give a paper at a statistical conference the next day. We were served dinner on trays. I had the aisle seat, and suddenly the flight attendant dropped a dinner tray upside down on my shoulder and onto my lap! The mashed potatoes and gravy burned me slightly and thoroughly soiled my shirt and pants. The flight attendant was very apologetic, helped me clean up, and assured me that she would give me a $5 coupon to get my suit cleaned.

I explained, "This is the only suit I have on the trip. Thank you, but I'm not interested in the five dollars. The important thing is to get my suit cleaned."

She told me, "Go to the ticket counter when you get off the plane and one of the agents will take care of you."

I went; at about 6:30 p.m. I spoke with an agent. "I really need to get my suit cleaned. It's the only one I have with me."

He was pleasant and asked, "Where are you staying?"

"The Radisson," I replied.

"They'll take care of you."

"Would you please call them and confirm that?" I asked.

He was gone for a while so I spread out the New York Times on the counter and read to pass the time. I was feeling relaxed, somehow knowing that everything would work out. I was enjoying my confidence in the process. When he came back, he had a slightly sheepish look and told me, "I'm sorry, but the people at the Radisson won't be able to help you."

I remained calm. Another agent said, "I think I know of a dry cleaners that's open this late," and went away.

I continued reading. She came back beaming. "The cleaners is on your way from the airport to the hotel. All you need to do is drop off the suit, check in, and get back to the cleaners before their eight o'clock closing time."

I explained to her, "I never check into a hotel in my underwear."

She went away again and I continued reading. I was still relaxed. Finally, I was introduced to a third agent. He would drive me to the hotel, I would check in, he would go to the room with me, I would give him my suit, and he would take it to the cleaners, wait while it was cleaned, and return it to me at the hotel. This is what we did; at 8:20 p.m., I had a clean suit.

I have told this story many times to illustrate the importance of being patient. Eventually I came to realize that I had been part of the solution. By being calm and relaxed, I expressed my confidence in the agents' ability to find a solution to my problem. Wordlessly, I kept telling them, "You can do it!" And they did. I was living out of the principle *everything turns out right . . . when you let it* long before I discovered it.

As this process was taking place, I didn't know what was "right." Part of the principle is that we don't know what is right for us in any particular experience. When we think we do, we are likely to push for that outcome, which gets in the way of "letting it"—repeat—*letting it* turn out right. Some people might decide that it would be "right" for them to be given a new suit (to compensate them for pain and suffering) and would negotiate very hard to get it. Their peace and joy would depend on getting a voucher for a new suit. Others might decide they deserved a free round-trip ticket to anywhere in the United States that the airline served and would negotiate very hard to get it. Their peace and joy would depend on getting a voucher for a round-trip ticket.

An important aspect of this principle is that we don't know ahead of time what is "right" for us, we don't have to push for our solution, and we'll recognize the "right" outcome when we see it. Allowing ourselves to recognize and accept the outcome as right is part of the process. This is true regardless of the outcome.

Consider the man who wants a free ticket to anywhere as compensation for his soiled suit. Let's suppose he does not get one. He could become enraged and not even get a clean suit, just the $5 voucher. I would like him to be able to step back from the event and see that the outcome was right for him, providing a wonderful opportunity for him to learn. Learn what? To live with more inner peace, with more forgiveness, with less fear. The payoff could be to avoid a stroke or heart attack at some later date.

The situation will only turn out right if he lets it. What does that mean? He must give up insisting on his solution. If the man who wants a free ticket doesn't allow himself to see that the outcome was right for him and doesn't learn, he will go through this again. That's not wrong, just painful and perhaps unhealthy. When he lives out of the belief that everything turns out right when he lets it, these episodes will diminish in the stress that they engender and in their frequency.

We will see in this book that we either succeed or we learn. That is, we get what we want—a clean suit with no hassle—or we discover that we don't need what we want. I could have gotten along without having the suit cleaned at the dry cleaners; I could have cleaned it as well as possible and still given the paper. We get what we want, or we **can** learn that we don't need what we want. Learning is optional and a highly desirable choice.

This principle is not based upon a belief in any grand plan, just a series of opportunities to learn, grow, and change. If we don't let it, if we insist on our solution ("I want a free ticket"), it won't turn out right in the sense that we will experience little peace, joy, and love. And if we react to all of our opportunities that way, our lives will be very stressful regardless of whether we get a new suit or a plane ticket.

The experience of a close friend of mine provides further insight into what's right. He flew to Munich on a Sunday on a business trip to meet with the executives of a large, highly respected German company, a prospective business partner. At baggage claim, he discovered that his bag had not arrived. Since he was wearing shorts and T-shirt, his first thought was that he'd have to go buy an outfit to wear the next day. He quickly learned that most stores, including all clothing stores, were closed on Sunday. Although he tried to figure out a way around it, in the end he went to his meeting in his shorts and T-shirt, explaining

. . . when you let it

somewhat awkwardly what had happened. The German executives, frequent travelers themselves, thought this was very funny and eventually settled down to a successful meeting. Some time later, my friend was back meeting with the same group and was treated like a minor celebrity, with lots of good-natured kidding about his showing up in a suit this time. Everything turned out right because my friend let it. He did not hide in his hotel room until the stores opened on Monday, as some would have done, which would have made him late for his meeting, thereby offending his hosts. His willingness to go to the meeting as he was demonstrated a personal strength that others appreciated. That helped the meetings turn out right.

THE FORCE FOR GOOD

The principle *everything turns out right . . . when you let it* is based upon a belief in a force or energy within us that we cannot control, but we can tap into. This energy has been called by many names: inner voice, subconscious, God, Holy Spirit, Guardian Angel, Jesus, Spirit Guide, Universe, Mary, Voice for God, Nature, Divine Energy, Allah, Buddha Nature, Higher Self, Conscience, Great Spirit, Divine Mind, and many others. Are these all the same entity? Perhaps, but we don't have to resolve that question. Instead, we can simply acknowledge the force for good in our lives. It is available to us both as guidance and energy, and we are responsible for bringing it into our consciousness. I will make references to this guidance and energy throughout the book, for they are the underpinnings of the principle. I will often refer to them as the Source. Do we need to acknowledge the force for good in our lives in order for this principle to work for us? No. I experienced it before acknowledging it; my life taught me that it was there.

It is helpful to understand this principle the way we understand gravity, which has been operating since time began. Newton discovered it in the seventeenth century, and ever since it has served as a framework for our understanding of how the world works. Knowing how gravity operates, we work with it and that knowledge makes our life simpler. But you don't have to believe in it to make gravity work for you. It's the same with *everything turns out right . . . when you let it.* Knowing how it operates, we can work with it, making our lives simpler, more effective, and more relaxed. *The principle employs a force or energy within ourselves that we do not control; it works regardless of whether we believe in the Source.*

I did not invent this principle; I simply re-discovered it. It's been there all along. In the second century AD, the Roman emperor Marcus Aurelius said, "Whatever happens at all happens as it should; thou wilt find this true, if thou shouldst watch narrowly."[1] I was paraphrasing this Stoic philosopher without even knowing it.

Vaclav Havel, poet and former President of the Czech Republic, wrote, "Hope is not the conviction that something will turn out well, but the certainty that something makes sense, regardless of how it turns out."

CHARLIE'S LAW™ POSTERS

Three weeks after my friend challenged me to come up with something better than Murphy's Law, he and I were back together. I told him about my discovery, and he loved it. We called it Charlie's Law™ and agreed that it deserved to be publicized.

My friend was excited about Charlie's Law™. When he heard someone mention Murphy's Law he would jump in and say something like, "Didn't you know? Murphy's Law has been repealed! It's been replaced by Charlie's Law™: *Everything turns out right . . . when you let it.*" Later he'd call me and tell me about the positive response he'd received.

. . . when you let it

To publicize the principle, we decided that I would make posters. For the posters, I wanted corollaries, aphorisms supporting the basic principle. They popped into my head surprisingly easily but the publication of the posters was a long, slow process. Over the course of about five years, I tried printing photographs on glossy paper; commissioning an artist to create a beautiful background; and printing the text from my computer, then copying it in black and white on poster board at a copy shop, and decorating the plain black and white posters by hand using colorful magic markers.

Nothing was satisfactory. The low point came about a year or so after I started distributing the decorated posters: the colors were fading badly. All this time I was thinking, "*Everything turns out right . . . when you let it.*" Then in 1997, a series of events in my life began which culminated in a breakthrough.

I Am Shown My Path

In the spring, I had a bout of asthma. I had experienced asthma symptoms on and off all my life, and this was a severe episode. When it was almost over, I reported to my doctor that everything was okay except when I played racquetball a burning sensation developed around my throat. He suggested that the discomfort could be from angina instead of asthma and referred me to a cardiologist. I took the treadmill stress test and flunked. I was advised to have an angioplasty, and I did, which led to the insertion of two stents to keep my coronary arteries open. My understanding of *everything turns out right . . . when you let it* is that we are either succeeding or learning. A diagnosis of heart disease didn't seem like success to me, so I lay on the hospital bed asking myself, "What am I supposed to be learning from this?" A small voice within answered, "Retire from your job and work on Charlie's Law™."

I briefly considered retiring and saw that I had a good job working with a lot of nice people, a job I liked and paid well. I was not ready to retire, although I was well past retirement age.

Three months later my symptoms returned. The healing tissue had surrounded and partially blocked one of the two original stents. The doctors recommended that it be drilled out and another stent inserted. This was done, and soon I was lying on the hospital bed asking myself, "What am I supposed to be learning from this?" A small voice within answered, "Retire from your job and work on Charlie's Law™."

I considered retiring a little more seriously than the first time and saw once again that I had a good job working with a lot of nice people, a job I liked and paid well. I was still not ready to retire.

A year later I was diagnosed with arrhythmia (I experienced what I called skipped heartbeats) and I was offered a pacemaker. It was put in place, and once again I was lying on the hospital bed asking myself, "What am I supposed to be learning from this?" The same answer came from a small voice within, "Retire from your job and work on Charlie's Law™." This time my inner guidance reminded me of the following story Sharon and I had heard when we were living in West Virginia several years earlier.

Zeke was a pious man, living in a "holler" (a narrow valley with hills rising abruptly on each side). It had been raining for some time and the creek bordering his property had overflowed its banks. A neighbor went by in a canoe and called out to the man who was sitting on the porch. "Come on, Zeke, get in. There's no telling how high this flood's going!"

"No thanks," Zeke replied, "I'll be all right. The good Lord will take care of me."

Some time later, the water had risen farther and the pious man had to go up to the second floor, where he sat on the roof of the porch, watching the creek rise. A distant neighbor appeared in his rowboat and called out to him. "Come on, get in the boat. The creek is still rising! You've got to hurry because this current is very strong."

"No thanks," replied Zeke, "That's okay. I'll be all right. The good Lord will take care of me." And the boat headed downstream.

. . . when you let it

The water rose very rapidly and soon the pious man was up on top of his house, straddling the roof with the water nearly reaching his feet. A rescue boat came by and the pilot called out, "Come on. I'll throw you a rope and pull you into the boat!" "No thanks," said Zeke, "That's okay. I'll be all right. The good Lord will take care of me." And the boat roared off downstream.

Just then, the man found himself in front of St. Peter. Zeke exclaimed, "What am I doing here? I thought the good Lord would save me!"

To which St. Peter replied, "Well, we sent you three boats."

In the hospital, I realized I had received my third "boat." I wasn't ready to meet St. Peter! A month later, I announced my retirement. Three messages were enough—I went into the poster business.

Since then, my heart has gotten steadily stronger and the "skipped beats" have virtually stopped. One interpretation of this is that the arrhythmia had done its job. It had gotten me to retire and go into the poster business, and so I could get along fine without it.

Inner guidance plays an important role for me. However, we are always free to choose not to turn to our Source for advice; also, we can ignore the guidance we get. If the guidance comes unbidden, as it often has with me, we can choose to ignore it. I have always chosen to follow my guidance, sooner or later.

BEING OPEN

A friend of mine is very much in touch with her spirituality. Over the past ten years or so she has been visited by crows. She sees them as instruments of communication from her Spirit Guides. A few months ago she called me to say, "I'm in a spiritual quandary. I can't figure it out. May I share it with you?"

"Of course," I said.

everything turns out right . . .

"It's about my crow," she began.

I said to myself, "I won't know what to tell her."

Then I thought, "And I will be open to receiving guidance."

I had known for years that many things in nature are catalysts for my friend finding guidance. It is a spiritual reality in her life, so I listened to her story.

"A few days ago a crow appeared, after my not seeing one for maybe six months. He sat on a branch just outside my kitchen window, at about eye level. In the past, he was always much higher up in the branches of a tree and far away. But this time he was sitting right at eye level, only ten feet away, swaying precariously on a thin branch! He looked directly into my eye with an intent gaze and then flew away. I was mesmerized. My physical body was frozen stiff. It was as if a bolt of energy was sent directly from the crow's eye to deep inside my gut. This was so intense and really scared me. I emotionally and physically ran. It was a profound spiritual experience. What is the message? I know it has great meaning for me, but I don't understand. What does it mean? I can't figure it out."

I allowed that to sink in for 10—20 seconds. Then, with no idea what I was driving at, and without thinking about it, the words came to me: "How would it feel if you gave the crow unconditional love?"

She responded by skirting the question, talking about the question, and not answering it. Indirectly, she seemed to be saying, "I can't give the crow unconditional love because it is a spiritual being, way up there, beyond my reach."

I responded with, "Maybe the message from the crow was that you and he are on the same level. He rested on the branch at eye level instead of up in a tree. So you two are on the same level spiritually."

"I know that intellectually, and it scares me," she replied. "I didn't get it deep inside me. Now I get it."

Suddenly she began crying, overwhelmed by the beauty and significance of it all.

. . . when you let it

My friend was observing the crow with her heart and soul. For my part, the critical step was that after I said to myself "I won't know what to tell her" I added, "And I will be open to receiving guidance." This allowed it to come. When the words came, "How would it feel if you gave the crow unconditional love?" I mulled them over for a few seconds, not knowing or understanding their meaning. I decided I wouldn't censor my inner guidance, and it turned out to be an answer my friend understood and valued.

A New Outlook

When we really get it that everything turns out right when we let it, the ups and downs of daily life have fewer downs and more ups, and the challenges that people or circumstances offer us are less formidable. The situations that used to threaten us no longer do.

The hospital experience of mine serves to illustrate this last observation. When I went to the hospital for the cardiologist to check on my "skipped heartbeats," he found that one chamber was operating out of sync with the other, causing irregular heartbeats. My at-rest heart rate was in the low to middle forties. I would need a lot more medicine to suppress the extra beats, but, as a side effect, the additional medicine would slow the heart rate still further. At 10:15 a.m., my cardiologist and his specialist in the heart's electrical system visited my bedside and suggested I be fitted with a pacemaker to maintain a good pulse rate while taking enough medicine to control the irregular heartbeats. The doctors explained, "You don't have to do it."

I asked, "When do I have to decide?"

"In the next 15 minutes, because we've made a reservation for you at eleven."

Despite the fact that I knew next to nothing about pacemakers, except for those warnings next to microwave ovens, and had certainly never thought of one for myself, I said, "Okay, let's do it."

Knowing that *everything turns out right . . .* helped a lot. I did not say to myself, "Everything turns out right . . . when you let it, and therefore I choose not to get a pacemaker." Instead, I followed my inner guidance to choose the pacemaker. I said, "Okay."

During the procedure, I was lying on the table, sedated but awake while the doctor was cutting and inserting the pacemaker and its wires. Suddenly, someone on the team muttered, "Oh shit!"

I did not panic. I chose to focus on . . . *when you let it.* That is, I thought it would be better not to ask about what happened and take the team's attention away from fixing it; I let the team do what it had to do. As I lay there, I thought about the Bill Cosby routine where he is in the dental chair and he says to the dentist, "Did I hear you say 'Oops'? . . . Why did you say 'Oops'? . . . I know what I mean when I say 'Oops'!" and so on. I remember lying there thinking that it was a very funny routine. And I just relaxed and made whatever the medical team was doing okay.

After I was out of the hospital and visiting the cardiologist on the first follow-up appointment, I asked about what I had heard. I was told that during the insertion of a wire intended for a vein, an artery had been accidentally punctured. Since the arteries and veins are packed close together, this sometimes happens. Because the wire was so small in diameter, no damage had been done. I saw that there had been a problem, and I had been part of the solution.

If these events had taken place in 1968 instead of 1998, I would have reacted differently. When asked to decide about having the pacemaker inserted, I would have resented being "put on the spot," negotiated for more time, and, initially, been unhappy regardless of my choice. When a glitch occurred in the procedure, I would have at least been worried, quietly insisting on an explanation of what had happened and what the medical team was going to do about it. I would have wanted to be in charge.

So, what is the meaning of *everything turns out right . . . when you let it?* It doesn't mean that it turns out the way we want it. To see how this principle works, we must step back and take a long view. Then we find that in every situation, we are either succeeding or learning.

SUCCESS AND LEARNING

When we are in a hurry, standing in a long line at the checkout counter, we're either succeeding or learning: we're succeeding in getting checked out quickly—perhaps because another cash register is opened and we are invited to be one of the first in the new line—or we're learning patience. When I am in such a line and the person in front of me seems agitated, I will say, "We're learning patience" in a cheery voice. Most of the time that person will make a lighthearted response, and his or her shoulders will drop.

Another illustration of succeeding and learning comes from when I was going home after visiting an out-of-state friend who had experienced a death in the family. It was Saturday afternoon, and I returned my rental car at the airport. When I got to the ticket counter, my wallet was gone, along with all my money, credit cards, and license. When I remembered paying the toll and fiddling with the wallet in my pocket, I became convinced that the wallet had slipped out and was wedged between the seat and the door. I went back to the rental car return area and asked the people there to check the car and get my wallet. They found no wallet. I immediately suspected someone had seen the wallet and decided it contained a lot of good things and held on to it. So we negotiated and the manager said he would make arrangements so that the wallet could be returned anonymously by the person who took it. The person could keep the money and just return the credit cards and papers. We did that, but still no wallet. At that point, time was running out for catching my flight back home so I left.

This was very upsetting to me. Having my personal belongings drifting around felt scary, like my life was out of control. The next morning I was to give a talk in church entitled *Looking at What Is*, based on a concept described by J. Krishnamurti, one of the leading thinkers of the twentieth century. On the plane from Newark to Charlotte, I had time to think about this and get in touch with the fact that not only did I want to look at what is—the simple facts of the matter in a detached way—but this was a great vehicle for my talk the next day.

Upon arriving in Charlotte, I called the banks and cancelled my credit cards and took all the necessary steps—as if it were someone else's wallet, that is, without emotional attachment. I learned a lot about "looking at what is" that evening, looking at things without judgment. I still don't know where the wallet went; I may have left it on the courtesy bus that took me to the airport. It doesn't matter, because I went through the process, which offered me an opportunity to learn a valuable lesson. The next day in my talk I told the story as an illustration of the value of looking at what is, looking at the lost wallet with detachment, without judgment, without an emotional involvement in the outcome, without the feelings of a victim, just watching the situation, and myself in it, as a movie or a play. *I was more effective in coping with adversity because I just looked at what is and responded to that.*

I have not always understood the twin opportunities known as "success" and "learning." The first time I asked a girl for a date after moving to a new town, I was turned down. This was not a success. The idea grabbed me: I must be an unattractive guy. I didn't know enough to ask myself, "What am I supposed to be learning from this?" If I had realized that this was a learning opportunity, I would not have been hurt, and I would have figured out a better way to develop a social life.

One of the things I learned from the writings of J. Krishnamurti is: "No one is doing it to me." If I'm being prevented from doing what (I think) I want to do, another person is usually involved, asking me or expecting me to do something

. . . when you let it

else. The person who is preventing me from doing what I planned to do is I. I will only give up my plans if I prefer to do what the other person has asked, and only then. The request of the other person is not the problem, it's the inner conflict between doing what I planned and maintaining my image as a nice guy by doing what the other person wants. This situation presents the opportunity to learn that going ahead with the plan and doing what has been requested are always healthy choices. The choice doesn't matter. What matters is choosing out of love for myself and for the other person. By choosing to follow my plan because I'm afraid the work will never get done or I'll never have time to myself, I'm putting stress on myself and on the other person. By choosing to give up my plan and do what I've been asked to do instead because I'm afraid the other person will think less of me or will retaliate sometime, I'm putting stress on myself and on the other person. By operating out of the principle *everything turns out right . . . when you let it,* I'll make my choice from a relaxed, centered place, and it will turn out right.

When I apply for a job, or someone else in my department is promoted, I'm either succeeding or learning. "Succeeding" implies I get the job, although that is not always the case. Learning means knowing I can do well without that job. A better job may be available, one more suited to my talent; maybe not getting the job opens up a whole new set of possibilities for me. This was indeed true for me when I didn't get the promotion I wanted.

I worked in the research department of a large oil company and was highly regarded. One of my co-workers was promoted to a job I wanted. I was keenly disappointed; if I had known it was a learning opportunity for me, it would have been much easier for me. Five years later, I realized that I didn't get the job because I didn't belong there. At that point, I listened to my inner guidance, let go, and flew, as described in Chapter 9. *Inner guidance is available and works when we listen, regardless of what we understand or believe about it.*

LET THE UNIVERSE DECIDE

For many years, a friend of mine has owned a rental property with two apartments. It was originally a one-family house and had been converted before my friend acquired it. She wasn't sure whether she wanted to put her time and energy into managing the property, so she called me to ask, "Right now I've had one apartment empty for many months and my other tenant is leaving the first of September. I've had an ad in the paper for the whole time and I haven't found a desirable tenant. I don't know whether to keep trying to find an appropriate tenant or to put the house up for sale. It could be converted back to a one family house. What spiritual principles could help me?"

I replied, "Let the Universe decide. Don't look for a 'sign' from the Universe. Set it up so that the Universe can decide and show you the decision. Set a time limit for getting a tenant. Then the force for good in your life, who knows what is for your highest good, can either bring you a tenant and you will keep renting, or not, and you will put it up for sale. You don't have to figure it out."

Soon after that she decided to sell it and on a Friday afternoon called a friend who is in real estate. She told him she wanted to sell the house and asked him to come look at it, preferably that afternoon. He was busy that day, and they made an appointment for Monday. That weekend, before she had a chance to list it with the realtor, she rented the whole house for two years! After reflecting on what happened, my friend commented, "Although I didn't realize it at the time, when I called my realtor friend, I let the Universe know that I was serious about selling if I didn't have a tenant. The Universe doesn't do anything until you take the first step."

. . . when you let it

Letting Go of Emotional Attachment
to the Outcome

One of the beauties of turning decisions over to the Source is that we can more easily let go of any emotional attachment to the outcome. At a very simple level, when we are entertaining visitors and planning outdoor activities, we could say, "If it doesn't rain, we'll do this, and if it rains, we'll do this other thing." Then, all we have to do is wait and see whether it rains; we are prepared. This is in contrast to, "Let's hope it doesn't rain; I don't know what we'll do if it rains," repeated frequently. Making this choice sets up a strong emotional attachment to the outcome when, in truth, all we want to know is that everything turns out right when we let it. Then it doesn't matter whether it rains.

I might hear, "But we reserved the shelter in the park six months ago; it can't rain." Yes, it can and, if it does, we can have a great time using our alternative plan. Doing our best and letting go insure that everything will turn out right.

. . . When You Let It

What does . . . *when you let it* mean? As illustrated in the account of the decision to have a pacemaker installed, it does not mean doing nothing. You don't sit around waiting for everything to turn out right. It does mean you actively create good in your life and choose not to have an emotional investment in the outcome. The expressions, "It's not fair!" and "Why me?" disappear from your vocabulary (if they ever were there). It means effortlessly doing your best at all times and then letting go. These are the key ingredients in this process. They enable you to hear your inner voice, trust it, use that guidance, and function with love.

At a practical level, . . . *when you let it* means giving up control, allowing your life to unfold, trusting that you are being guided toward experiences of love, peace, and joy. "But," you might say, "I've tried that; it doesn't work." Look again at those situations and see whether you gave up control entirely, whether you were just watching your life unfold. Then look at the outcomes for signs of love, peace, joy, and *learning*. Look at them in the light of my experience with the lost wallet and my friend's experience without his luggage. When we let it, we got better results. People do not perform well when they are nervous. If we're worried or fearful, we will not perform as well, either. *If we know that everything turns out right, we'll have more loving experiences.*

Decisions become easier when we live out of an understanding of this principle. We are familiar with easy decisions: "It's a no-brainer!" Hard decisions are the ones involving two attractive choices. Very hard decisions are those involving two equally attractive choices appearing to take us on divergent paths—perhaps one requires a move to a faraway country and the other means staying home. And both choices look very good in their own way. Some people approach the situation analytically, assigning point values to each of several attributes, determining the extent to which each alternative demonstrates that attribute, and then choosing the alternative with the most points. That works very well for many people. When we accept the principle that *everything turns out right . . . when you let it* and are left with two or more alternatives that seem equally attractive, we see that either of them will do. We can set aside any feelings of apprehension about making a mistake because we cannot make a mistake, we can only learn. Then we can choose the one that pleases us the most. We will be one step closer to experiencing greater joy and confidence. Easy decisions bring us joy. The following story illustrates these points.

A nephew of mine was completing a fellowship in Sports Medicine and had to choose between two attractive offers. He and his wife tabulated pros and cons, weighting the attributes for their importance. When their list was complete, they tallied the result and found the winner. But wait! "The winner" didn't feel right; it didn't match their intuition. The couple reflected on the issues, got in touch with their inner guidance, and saw that the other offer provided intangibles beyond the professional opportunity. They then chose

. . . when you let it

the other offer and it immediately felt right.   And several years later, they continue to feel they made a good choice.

Alan Watts wrote, "Spiritual awakening is the difficult process whereby the increasing realization that everything is as wrong as it can be flips suddenly into the realization that everything is as right as it can be. Or better, everything is as It as it can be."[2]

Seeing that *everything turns out right . . . when you let it,* living it, and owning it, constitute major steps in spiritual awakening.

How About You?

How can you use this idea to move from where you are to a place of greater joy and confidence? I suggest that being loving and compassionate is our natural state. Every time you don't feel that way, you have an opportunity for growth. Listen quietly and allow yourself to hear: *everything turns out right . . . when you let it.* Don't say it to yourself. Instead allow it to come from your Source. Then take a deep breath, relax, and let go. The stress will subside, maybe only a little at first and maybe only briefly, and you will handle the situation better. Don't practice it as a drill; just let it come to you. You will be given many opportunities to learn; you will be amazed at how many opportunities will come to you. As you keep practicing, your response will get easier. As it becomes part of your natural thinking, the opportunities will diminish, and you will be living with greater joy and confidence. *Be in touch with your loving, compassionate nature.*

The Way Things Are

The discomfort that triggers distress typically happens when we are seeing or hearing something that does not conform to our picture of the world. It can arise at home; at work; on the road between them; on the phone with friends, relatives, customers, clients, or solicitors; at a soccer match; in fact, anywhere. We want something to be one way, and we find that it's another way.

everything turns out right . . .

We want a promotion, which we think we've earned, and it goes to someone else. We want our spouse or significant other to do more of the chores that are being shared. We want our children to behave in a certain way, and they don't. We want the other drivers on the road to drive safely and considerately (the way we do), and they don't. We want the government not to do some of the things that it does. When you say "I want . . ." or "I *wish* . . . ," allow *everything turns out right . . . when you let it* to slip into your consciousness and put you at ease.

The countless minor and major clashes between the way life is and the way we want it to be are the foundation stones for inner conflict and outward anger. These clashes are an endless series of opportunities to move to greater joy and confidence. Let the distress you feel be a catalyst for transforming the situation from frustration to peace. Everything is okay just the way it is. As each of these situations is played out, we see the truth of this more clearly. We see that each of them is a learning opportunity through which we can work peacefully for change. *Every irritation is an opportunity for growth.*

What are you to learn? Perhaps to be more forgiving of the people who create situations that upset or challenge you. To be more forgiving of yourself. To understand that, at a deeper level, there is nothing to forgive because no one is doing it to you, it only feels that way sometimes. To act out of love in all situations, because the people who are creating situations that upset or challenge you will benefit from your love.

When someone is fired, starving, or dying, is this because they did not follow the right process? NO! That's just the way life is. How can you relate to those things? With love and compassion, which are parts of your natural state. You are not a blank slate; love and compassion are a part of each one of us. You can help yourself by being in touch with, aware of, this aspect of yourself. As you do, these feelings will grow. Extend love and compassion first to the dying and later to the survivors. It may take a lot of time, but everything will turn out right for the survivors when they let it.

. . . when you let it

Please read the following very slowly. *Everything turns out right . . . when you let it.* Allow it to enfold you. Sink into it. Reflect on it. Without questioning it or judging it, just let it be there for you. That's the way life is. Be open to the truth of it and, as you read this book, let yourself see that this principle describes the way the world works. Whenever you feel perplexed or upset, you can repeat it silently to yourself, using it as a simple reminder that everything is okay.

Summary

◊ Everything turns out right . . . when we let it.

◊ We don't know what is right for us in any particular situation.

◊ We don't have to push for our solution.

◊ We get what we want or we learn.

◊ Look at what is.

◊ Be in touch with your loving, compassionate nature.

◊ Inner guidance is available.

◊ Recognize the force for good in your life.

◊ Give up control.

2

If You Need Something,
It Will Come to You

"We never understand how little we need in this world."
—James Barrie

S tarting in 1982 with my decision to separate from my first
wife, my life has taken many twists and turns, more than
would be useful to recount here. However, parts of that
history illustrate the idea that I got the things I needed for my
spiritual development even though I didn't know at the time
what they were.

My decision to separate was prompted by inner guidance,
and it was a watershed experience. Within weeks of making that
decision, while flying from Tampa to New York City, I met a
woman with a great deal of inner strength and wisdom. She
introduced me to the writings of J. Krishnamurti and the idea of
taking EST training, as she had done. EST was an organization
offering personal development training, the word standing for
Erhard Seminar Training and in Latin for *it is*. She had taken a
two-weekend program that was intense and confrontational. I
later did the same. I needed someone to jump-start me in my
spiritual development, and she was the one.

Two months later, I met another woman on a flight from Roanoke to NYC who was an EST graduate and a member of an EST support group that met not far from Roanoke. After I moved to Roanoke, she introduced me to her husband and EST friends. I was being guided to take that training, which I did. Although I didn't like the way they conducted the training, it reinforced J. Krishnamurti's teachings for me and opened up some new ideas for personal development.

At about that same time, I met Sharon at the Unitarian Church and she led me to explore two other religions. She subsequently introduced me to *A Course in Miracles*, which became the cornerstone of my spiritual awareness.

These three women, and other teachers as well, helped me to realize who I am. I needed all three of these women; they came, and I listened.

Although this sounds very simple and smooth, it was not. Relatively early in this transition I read an article about stress factors. Separation and divorce, a new job, and a move of 750 miles combined to put me well above the critical stress level and to the top of the chart. And through it all, I was experiencing spiritual growth.

WHAT DO WE NEED?

What do we need to live a fulfilling life? Food, clothing, and shelter, as well as emotional well being, loving relationships, spiritual growth, and stimuli for personal and professional growth.

The good news is that we don't have to go after the things we need; they will come to us. How will they? By a series of everyday miracles; I'll soon give a few examples.

Let's consider the significance of this principle. Does it mean that we will get what we want? No. It means the things that come to us are the things we need. In fact, we can identify our needs by the things we get, the things that come to us. Instead of deciding what we want or even what we think we need, we can open ourselves to the good that surrounds us. Then we can look at what comes into our lives and say, "Oh, that's what I need; that's what I'm supposed to be doing (when we get a new job or a new challenge)," or, "That's what I'm supposed to be working on."

Am I suggesting that it's not a good idea to want anything? Not at all. Once we accept the idea that what we need will come to us, we can desire, or wish to have, something, anything. And we can pursue our desires without anxiety because we know we will get what we need even if we don't get what we want.

EXERCISE:
A MEDITATION ON GETTING WHAT YOU NEED

Many people find it is easier to accept that they will get what they need than to see that their loved ones will get what they need. These people have a loving, protective, perhaps anxious attitude towards their loved ones—children, spouse, siblings, parents, partners, relatives, and friends. They want good things for their loved ones and that's wonderful. And it will help these people and their loved ones to know that they all get what they need.

Please do this: After you read this paragraph, put the book aside, close your eyes, take a deep breath, and let it go slowly. Repeat this until you feel a deep sense of relaxation. In this relaxed state, hear the following words: "If you need something, it will come to you, and if the people you care about need something, it will come to them." Stay with those words.

How do you feel? Lighter? Less anxious? Or not? In a minute, I'm going to ask you to do the exercise again, but first let's deal with the question, "How do you know that if you need something it will come to you?" The answer, which may surprise you, is simple: *Because it always has come to you!*

Think about it. You have progressed as far as you have in life because you have gotten what you needed: food, clothing, shelter, money, lack of money, lessons, opportunities for spiritual growth, friends, loving relationships, jobs, unemployment, and difficult relationships—just what you needed, exactly when you needed it.

Simple Examples of Getting What I Needed

Without always being aware of it, I've always gotten what I needed. In infantry basic training at Fort Dix, NJ, lying in my sleeping bag on the snow, I was not aware of it. My experience would have been easier for me if I had. In addition to the sleeping bag, I had winter clothing, a pup tent, and a full stomach each night. That was more than necessary, even though it wasn't what I wanted. The day I left my job to go into the U.S. Army, a co-worker wished me well and said, "It's a good thing to have been through." He was right. I matured, read a lot, spent a year in Japan, and, qualified for the G. I. Bill and its graduate school financial assistance. I received some of the basic building blocks of my adult life.

After being blessed with the principle, *Everything turns out right . . . when you let it,* I needed corollaries. And they came. Each time I saw a demonstration of the principle, the corresponding corollary appeared in my head. I now have over thirty. Many of the stories in this book evoked the corollaries that are now chapter headings. I needed them to illustrate the principle and they came.

When I was about 11 years old, one of my mother's friends, an avid tennis player, bought a new tennis racquet and gave me her old one. She also gave me a set of worn tennis balls that were still usable, and she continued to do that for a few years. I had access to free tennis courts in the neighborhood. My father was a good tennis player, and we had a cup he had won, although he had not played in many years. And I wanted to be like Dad. My family had little money so the gift of the tennis racquet was important to me; without it I wouldn't have taken up that sport, at least not then. I played fairly regularly for the next 50 years and added squash and racquetball to my activities. I needed a tennis racquet to begin a lifetime of fun, and I got it.

. . . when you let it

Someone Else's Example

A realtor was visiting a house that had recently been put on the market. In the course of her inspection, she saw a *Charlie's Law*™ poster and was fascinated by it. Before she left, she had memorized a few corollaries. As time went by, she wished she had one of those posters.

Many months later she held an open house near the one where she had seen the poster. One of the neighbors dropped in just to see what the house was like. When the neighbor said where she lived, the agent recognized it as the house with the poster and told the neighbor how much she liked the poster, quoted a few corollaries, and asked if the neighbor knew how she could get a copy. Yes indeed! The neighbor's husband was involved in the *Charlie's Law*™ poster business, with a stack of new posters at home. The neighbor went home, got two posters, and made a sale to a very happy customer. Apparently, the realtor needed it, and it came to her, hand delivered. (A sequel to this story appears in Chapter 9.)

The converse of that story involves a friend of ours. When he saw the posters, he liked them and decided *not* to order any. He said, "If I need one, it will come to me." (A few years later, his wife bought a poster.)

We Get What We Need
even Though We Don't Want It

A young engineer was not performing well, and he was assigned to me to help him improve his performance or be let go. He did not perform well because he did not do his work. Instead, he spent a lot of time talking to the mail girl who worked in our department. After counseling him unsuccessfully on several occasions, I recommended that he be fired and he was. Six months later, he sent me a Christmas card with a note saying how much he appreciated what I had done for him and how much he was enjoying his new job. He didn't *want* a new job, but he needed it.

EXERCISE: LEARNING THE PRINCIPLE

In order to get clearer that if you need something, it will come to you, please do the previous exercise again. After you read this paragraph, put the book aside, close your eyes, take a deep breath, and let it go slowly, and relax. Repeat this until you feel a deep sense of relaxation. In this relaxed state, hear the following words. "If you need something, it will come to you, and if the people you care about need something, it will come to them."

Whenever you sense a lack of something for yourself or someone you care about, listen to your inner voice saying, "If you need something, it will come to you." or "If they need something, it will come to them." Do this because you know it's true, because it always has been true, and it always will be true. Do it because that sense of lack tells you that you've momentarily forgotten this principle, and you want to make it part of your awareness again.

THIS PRINCIPLE APPLIES TO EVERYONE

How does this apply to the poor people of this country? Just the way it applies to everyone else. They want things better for themselves and their loved ones: more and better food, clothing, shelter, security, education, recreation . . . everything. We want these things for them, too. They are working as hard as they can to get what they want. Like everyone, they are getting what they need. This may sound simplistic because we know many poor people in this world are sick, starving, and dying. Others are abused and mistreated. Does everything turn out right for all of these people? I believe so, and my readings of *A Course in Miracles*[3] and *Conversations with God*[4] support my belief.

How does the principle of this chapter apply to the very rich? One might wonder whether people who are very rich really need the money that comes into their lives. The answer is "Yes," and their challenge is to know why they need it. Some

. . . when you let it

rich people use their money to get more money, some to help others, some to enrich the lives of their families, some for a lavish life style, and some for philanthropy such as support for the homeless and the arts. It would be appropriate for all these people to ask themselves, "What do I need my wealth for? What is my vision that I need my money to fulfill?"

The money that comes to the rich is what they need, and it is for them to figure out what the need is, just as it is for everyone else. We are all "rich" in the sense that we get what we need. Everyone must figure out what to do with the money and talent they have and with the physical, intellectual, and spiritual gifts they've been given. They must do this in order to realize themselves fully, to be fulfilled, and to share in the joy of the Universe.

How does the principle *If you need something, it will come to you* fit with the principle, *Everything turns out right . . . when you let it?* Realizing that we get what we need is one of the consequences of knowing everything turns out right. We couldn't experience everything turning out right if we didn't get what we need. The purpose of this chapter is to demonstrate that we get what we need even when it does not feel that way.

From time to time, someone will exclaim, "I don't need this!" It may be the result of a confrontation at home, at work, on the road, at the mall, on the ball field, or any of many other places. Or it could be from some news from the IRS, an insurance company, or an auto mechanic. The statement is not true. Of course you need it, otherwise it wouldn't have happened. It would be much more accurate to say, "I don't want this," and then quickly add, *"But why do I need this?"* Or, as described in Chapter 1, "What am I supposed to be learning from this?"

A CAREER

I grew up during the Depression. My family was poor, and my parents' highest values for me were education and a well-paying career. From the time I was about nine years old and had demonstrated a proficiency in arithmetic, my parents told me I was to go to college, become an engineer, and go to work for some good company for the rest of my working life. I did go to college and get an engineering degree but, after I graduated, my career has been made up of a series of unexpected gifts.

I was employed professionally every day for 49½ years. But, instead of working for one company, I worked for eight plus the U.S. Army, and I had my own consulting business twice. All but one of my job changes happened the same way: I received one job offer and took it. Each of the jobs was better than the last, personally, professionally and/or financially. Each of these changes contributed to, and was necessary for, my personal growth.

In the table below, I have outlined my career, since it illustrates the principle of this chapter. I didn't know enough to pursue the things that I needed for my growth. Under "Personal Development," the normal type represents what I thought I needed; the *italic type* describes what was actually going on. These items illustrate the principle that we can identify our needs by the things we get, the things that come to us.

Looking at this brief history, we see that going to graduate school was obviously part of my career path, I just didn't know about it until I got there. My U.S. Army tour showed me to be much more capable than my slightly above-average undergraduate record revealed. I wanted to go to graduate school to establish a better academic record and take advantage of the fact that it was free through the G. I. Bill. Being a consultant, both within my organization and as an independent, was an essential part of my career path, without me knowing it. The week I moved to Roanoke, Virginia, my future wife Sharon did too; I didn't know that either. We met and married, and each of us has been an enormous help to the other. When I joined the chemical company in 1992, I had no idea that my new job would give me an opportunity to move to the Tampa Bay area and be close to my two daughters.

The main point regarding these career developments is that I didn't know the things I needed, but I got them anyway.

. . . when you let it

PROFESSIONAL DEVELOPMENT	PLANNED DEVELOPMENT	GIFTED DEVELOPMENT
Sales/marketing job.	My first "real" job.	
Technical sales job.	Court and marry my first wife.	
Job in manufacturing and engineering for a large oil company.	Obtain financial security and job satisfaction.	
Draftee in the U.S. Army.	Fulfill my legal obligation.	*Become acquainted with a very different culture (Japan). Qualify for the GI Bill (federal funds) for graduate school.*
Full-time graduate student.	Take advantage of the GI Bill.	*Create future career opportunities. Learn more about how to think.*
Research and development chemical engineer for large oil company.	Obtain financial security and professional recognition. Design a house and have it built, fulfilling a childhood dream.	*Fulfill my parents' dream for my career. Become an in-house consultant to prepare for a consulting career.*
Independent consultant.	Make more money.	*Give up my conventional life and support system.*
General Manager for a small research and development company.	Maintain financial security. Get divorced.	*Meet Sharon, court and marry her; begin rapid spiritual growth.*
College professor.	Maintain financial stability; achieve more spiritual growth.	*Develop a new area of technical expertise for future consulting.*

PROFESSIONAL DEVELOPMENT	PLANNED DEVELOPMENT	GIFTED DEVELOPMENT
In-house consultant for medium-sized chemical company.	More professional opportunities and recognition. Maintain financial security.	*Move to Tampa Bay area to be close to my daughters and grandchildren.*
Retired. Consultant.	Publish posters.	*Professional satisfaction from consulting; financial security.*

Fortunately, I accepted them although sometimes very slowly, as in the story of the three heart procedures told in Chapter 1. The following is another illustration of getting what I needed and twice failing to recognize it.

It's Okay to Be a Slow Learner

I taught a course in Research and Development (R&D) Management for the American Institute of Chemical Engineers (AIChE) three or four times a year for 18 years. At the end of that time, because of my job change, I told the man who managed these courses I would be leaving. He was disappointed and wanted me to continue. I agreed to teach for one more year and then find my own replacement. At the time I made the commitment, I had no idea who that person might be.

A graduate school friend became Vice President of R&D for a nationally known process company and was a client of mine at one time. The Christmas after I said I'd find my replacement for AIChE, we received his family's newsletter along with their Christmas card. It was in the form of a newspaper with columns of text, headlines, and photos. I was busy the day it arrived and just glanced admiringly at the great format.

. . . when you let it

A few days later, Sharon showed the newsletter to me and told me that my friend had retired and was doing R&D management consulting. I thought to myself, "That's great!" A few months later, another friend of mine put me back on our graduate school's mailing list and, as a result, I received a copy of the Engineering bulletin which included a short item about my friend's retiring and going into the R&D management consulting business.

At that moment, I finally got it: he was going to be my replacement. I wrote to him and he accepted. AIChE was happy to have him, and I had fulfilled my commitment. In truth, I didn't really find him; the Universe presented him to me *three times,* and I finally recognized that he was the one. If you need something, it will come to you, even if you don't recognize it, as with the boats coming to the man sitting on his front porch in the pouring rain (see Chapter 1).

RELATIONSHIPS

All of us have relationships with various people—immediate and extended family members, other loved ones, friends, co-workers, and others. These people bring us what we need—someone for us to love and to love us. My highest goal is to be a loving person and, without relationships, I will not fully experience love. I could still talk about love, read about it, watch television programs and movies about it, love from afar, and extend love to people I hear about, but I feel that we need actual relationships to fully realize ourselves as loving individuals.

For our personal development, we also need people to push our buttons and challenge us. Luke recounts for us that Jesus told a great multitude, "Love your enemies, do good to those who hate you . . . If you love those who love you, what credit is that to you? Even sinners love those who love them . . . But love your enemies, do good to them, and lend to them without expecting to get anything back. Then your reward will be great, and you will be sons of the Most High."[5]

So we need our "enemies." How else can we continue to develop our loving kindness? We need tough opponents to sharpen our skills, just as great athletes do.

WHAT ABOUT YOU?

You need all the relationships you have. *If you need something, it will come to you.* As we discovered earlier in this chapter, you can identify your needs by the things you get, the things that come to you. This is also true of your relationships. They are there just for you, the loving ones, the extremely difficult ones, and all those in between. The loving ones teach us gratitude and humility; keep them and enjoy them. The extremely difficult ones, with people who may hate us or scorn us, teach us unconditional love. Allow them to nurture your highest self.

Think about some occasion when you have been angry or upset about something going on around you or immediately in front of you. It might have been someone cutting in front of you on the highway or maybe tailgating dangerously closely; an edict from the boss; a burned dinner; a bad call from the ref; or a slight from a relative or a close friend—any of those will do. Or think of one that has special significance to you. Allow yourself to feel the anger, resentment, or frustration you have felt before. Own those feelings.

Now think about another time when none of these things was bothering you. Notice that you immediately feel lighter, more peaceful, and happier. Clearly, you feel better when nothing is bothering you, and you would like to feel that way all the time.

Where do these negative feelings come from? From the part of us harboring some kind of resentment or ill feeling. Those feelings are there, waiting to take over. We don't have to know why we have these feelings; it's enough to know that we do. We need reminders that they are there. We *need* someone cutting in front, the occasional burned dinner, etc., to remind us that we are not at peace with ourselves. Then what? When we feel the tightness in our stomach, shoulders, neck or jaw, we can say, "Thanks, I needed that," because it's true. For our personal development, we must practice letting go of our negative responses. We can't let go very well in a vacuum, when nothing is bothering us. When we let go as part of our every-day challenges, we get better and better at it, until nothing bothers us. That is the goal.

Think of someone cutting in and out of the traffic at rela-tively high speeds. The driver gets ahead of you. Say, "Thanks, I needed that." Then forgive him, bless him, and relax, knowing that he will be gone in less than a minute because he is in a *big* hurry. Then you can continue unimpaired. By doing this with every upset every day, the negative feelings will lose their power, and a sense of well being and forgiveness will gradually take over.

Peace will come to you.

Summary

◇ If you need something, it will come to you.

◇ We get what we need, even when we don't want it.

◇ When something unexpected comes to you, figure out what you need it for. Then use it.

◇ Our loved ones are getting what they need, too.

◇ We need people to push our buttons in order for us to continue to grow.

3

When Faced with
a Difficult Task,
Start

"You don't have to get it right, you just have to get it going."
—Anonymous

Clearly, if we know everything is going to turn out right, the "difficult task" becomes quite manageable, and we will not hesitate to start. We might even be enthusiastic.

This is the message I have needed the most. Many times when doing a task, assignment, or project, I have the energy and creativity to complete it. It's getting started that can be a challenge.

A DIFFICULT TASK

What is a difficult task? One that prompts the reaction in you, "I don't want to do it." You might be feeling disinterested, frustrated, inadequate, incapable, angry, or overextended. You might combine those feelings with the idea that you are doing more than your share in a marriage or in a relationship, on a work team, as a caregiver or a community service volunteer. A new task is just "too much." You might see it as a boring, tedious job, beneath your ability; or without sufficient rewards, financial or personal. You might be afraid you lack the necessary skills, energy, and commitment to do it. Any of these could lead to an interesting discussion, but none of these issues matters.

The perception that *you have to do it* makes the task difficult. Actually, you don't have to do it, but for all practical purposes you do. You know when you have to do it: when you're the only one available, the only one qualified, the only one "willing," the only one who will get it done, because everyone is counting on you to do it, or for some other compelling reason.

SOME DIFFICULT TASKS

Let's look at some difficult tasks and describe why they are perceived to be difficult in order to see what's going on in our lives.

1. Painting the house. What makes it difficult? Here's what Rob says: *It's a dull, boring job. Scraping and getting the surfaces ready to prime requires strenuous effort. The weather is already pretty warm and I'll have some hot days with lots of sweat before the job is done. Sure, I'll use one of those electric scrapers to remove most of the old paint, but to get down into the corners, I'll need a handheld scraper and an all-out effort. To paint a house requires a lot of attention to detail. The last time I did it, I made a lot of mistakes and spent hours and hours fixing them. I'm not good at this. I don't paint often enough to be good at it. I'm not a professional painter. If I had a better job—one paying more money—I would hire someone to paint the house. Jack (up the street) never paints his house. He's had it done twice in the last 8 years, and he goes off and plays tennis. Great exertion in the hot sun is a lot different when you have a tennis racquet in your hand instead of a scraper. Paul (also up the street) on the other hand, loves this stuff. He's always out building, remodeling, or repairing something, even in the hottest weather. I'm just not like him. And besides, the house doesn't look too bad. If the in-laws weren't coming, we could put it off for another year, at least until fall. That's a much better time to paint outdoors. But my wife won't let me get away with postponing the job, and she's right. The wood is beginning to show in spots.*

What makes this painting job so difficult? Rob. His attitude. He's feeling sorry for himself.

2. Performing a job assignment when you are the only one in the company who can do it. Hiring a consultant is not an alternative because you were hired to do this kind of work. The assignment is in Teheran, Iran, and you are the only one who can speak Farsi, the local language. The technical aspects of the task are interesting and challenging. What makes it difficult?

Jim says: *Here's what I think. After I do all the work, nothing will come of it. I've been through this before, and that's how it's always turned out. After all the work is done, we'll end up with no agreement, no sale, no contract. They'll pay for my work, but overall it's a waste of the company's time, the client's money, and my talent. And speaking Farsi is not important. All the discussions are conducted in English. The management's just looking for an excuse to give me a job nobody wants. Nobody wants to leave his or her family for months at a time. I wish the client wouldn't keep asking for me.*

What makes this task so difficult? Fear of failure is a likely reason. If there were a history of technical and financial success in these dealings, an assignment in Teheran on the exact same project would be stimulating and exciting.

3. Picking up the children far across town for the third week in a row when four people are responsible for doing it. Two of them have never picked up the children; only Rebecca and Teresa have. Rebecca received the message this afternoon and the children will be waiting until she arrives. Why is this task difficult?

Rebecca says: *They are taking advantage of me. They must know I want the best for my children and will do what's needed to care for them. The other two are willing to just sit back and let me (and Teresa) do all the work. I'm very busy! And waiting until the last minute is so rude! I hate to let them get away with doing nothing.*

What makes this task difficult? The perception of lack of appreciation for what Rebecca and Teresa are doing. The feeling of being trapped by one's own standards. Being on a team with two players who are not playing.

4. Breaking painful news. The news could be about the death of a loved one, a medical diagnosis, laying off an employee, a separation or divorce. Why is breaking the news difficult?

Dan says: *Because the news is painful. I don't want to inflict pain on anyone. If it's the death of my loved one, I just can't bear it. Why do these things happen? If it's the death of someone else's loved one, it's almost as difficult. A diagnosis of many forms of cancer, Lou Gehrig's disease, Parkinson's disease, Lupus, or some other illnesses seems like a death sentence. I don't want to deliver it.*

Diane says: *When I had to lay off good, loyal, skillful employees simply because of poor management decisions, it hurt me a lot. I saw this coming a year ago. The people running this company could have known not to hire more people and not to replace people who retired or left for other jobs. But now I'm stuck with the mess they've made.*

Rachel says: *Explaining to the children that Daddy left us and we were on our own was so hard. I had known this for a whole week, all the time trying to summon up the courage to tell them. And when I told my parents, the pain was unbearable. I've failed myself, I've failed the children, I've failed.*

What makes breaking the news so difficult? We want the news to be different. We don't want to lose family, friends, employees, or a spouse, and we don't want to break our promises. We have a picture of how the future is going to unfold: everyone leading a long healthy life, retiring with a good pension, living happily ever after, and dying while peacefully asleep. The task of breaking bad news doesn't fit our picture. No one wants to be the bad guy. We didn't sign up for this.

IDENTIFYING RESISTANCE

The tasks aren't difficult, we are. Our resistance is what makes a task difficult. We have within us the energy to do what we want

. . . when you let it

to do. Adrenaline flows and allows a person of ordinary strength to lift a car to save the life of a child. Energy flows when we are doing what we want to do. Just notice the difficulties and allow them to fade away. The difficulties are captured in the answers to the following question.

WHAT AM I AFRAID OF?

Painting. Rob's afraid he won't look good. Everyone knows he doesn't like to work on the house so, if he paints his house, he thinks the neighbors will know he can't afford to hire a painter, that he doesn't have enough money.

Job assignment. Jim's afraid he's not respected. He's had this kind of assignment before and it has never worked out. How many more dead ends can he go down before he's fired? Nobody envies him for getting these jobs.

Picking up the children. Rebecca's afraid she is not appreciated. She thinks that if she and Teresa keep picking up the children, the other two will never do their share and she doesn't want to be saddled with this forever. She thinks, "My time is valuable too!"

Breaking the news. Dan is afraid of the reaction he'll receive. He's afraid he won't be able to cope with all the emotions that will come up, the tears, anger, even rage. He doesn't know how he can handle them.

Diane's afraid the people who are being laid off will have trouble finding jobs. Besides, they are her support system; you can't be a manager without people to manage, so she needs them. And she and the others who are left will have to do the work that was done by the people who were laid off. They will have to work harder although they're already working too much overtime. Can she do it?

Rachel is afraid for her children and herself. They were managing well enough before this happened, but now what? Where will the money, time, and quality time with the children come from? How can she spare the children's feelings? How can she handle it all?

everything turns out right . . .

A DIFFERENT LOOK

Painting. Rob can help himself by realizing that if another person interprets his house painting as a sign of lack of money, the problem lies within that person. Rob doesn't need to choose that interpretation. "Looking good," one of Rob's concerns, is in the eye of the beholder. Rob's perception of Rob is what matters. When he sees himself looking good, the task will no longer be difficult. The difficulty will fade when he has a (power) scraper and a ladder and when he gets to *start!* He could even get satisfaction out of doing it.

Job assignment. Jim's opinions of himself and his work are blocking his appreciation of his assignment. He can enjoy it for what it is: challenging work for a client who keeps asking for him. A healthy respect for the client will help him to have that perspective. When Jim reviews how the previous assignments went and how he can make this one better, he will create a different atmosphere for himself. To move ahead, he must embrace this assignment and *start!*

Picking up the children. When Rebecca is aware of how much she and the children enjoy each other during their trip home, she will see that she is appreciated a lot. She is not doing this for the other parents; she's doing it for the children and herself. She doesn't know the other two families or what their circumstances are. Clearly, picking up the children is a difficult task for them, too. If Rebecca knew them better, she might appreciate them the way she wants to be appreciated. Today, to get in touch with how much she and the children enjoy each other, she must *start!*

Breaking painful news. The people to whom Dan brings the news need his love and compassion. He doesn't have to do anything, just be there, with a hug and a soft word. He doesn't have to handle the emotions, just let them be, for the others, and for himself. He can let go of his resistance and see himself as a comforter when he gets to *start!*

Diane can help the people to whom she is conveying the news by shifting her perception from "they will have trouble finding jobs" to "they are good people, good workers and they will get good jobs, maybe better jobs, quickly." By seeing herself in this role, she will help herself. When she accepts that the people who remain will not be able to do all that had been done before, her fear of not getting the work done in the future will slowly melt away. All she needs to do is *start!*

Rachel is trapped by her visions of her failure. But it is not her failure. The children sense something is wrong, and they don't know what. Her task is to do something loving for the children: tell them their father has left, *nothing is wrong*, they are okay, all of us are okay, she loves them, he loves them, and they will be taken care of. Her task—to extend love to and reassure the children—will become clear as soon as she *starts!*

A Closer Look: What Can We Learn from This?

Painting. Rob can look at what is. His house needs painting now, before any serious damage occurs. He and his wife don't want to spend the money to hire someone to do the painting. He can do it, and so he will.

Job assignment. The decision for Jim to go to Teheran is between his company and the client. The client is important and his company wants to keep them happy. He is highly regarded and part of his job is to find out what he needs to do to end up with a sale and a long-term contract. He is not a victim; he is a participant.

Picking up the children. The children are always glad to see Rebecca. She is not the driver; she's the bringer of stability, love and joy into their lives.

Breaking the news. For Dan, the very qualities that make breaking the news seem like a difficult task are the ones that make him the right one for it. He can help the bereft just by being compassionate and loving.

Diane can acknowledge that the management didn't want the layoffs either; they would much rather have a highly prosperous company. All the employees share the responsibility for the health of the company.

Rachel can realize that what she thought were her failures are the things she can learn from. She has done the best she could. Her family life needs to be rebuilt; she can take this opportunity to shape their lives differently, to fill them with more love and joy.

These people will benefit from seeing their circumstances differently.

START

Nothing is wrong with you. You have nothing to be afraid of. You can do what you need to do. You will be given help.

Listen to the loving whisper, "Start." Allow yourself to hear it. This is your key to a different life experience, a series of different life experiences, a different life.

How could that be? "Start" seems like such a small thing. It isn't. It's often the point at which we are stuck. We need to be moving to use the available guidance. A ship needs to be moving in order to be steered. If the engine stops or the sails are down, the forward motion stops. When that happens, the rudder, which can still be moved, has no effect because water is not flowing across its surfaces. The ship could have the most advanced rudder system available, and we still wouldn't be able to steer it. The same is true for all of us. We have guidance, which is our advanced rudder system, available to us all the time. It has no effect, though, if we are not moving; once we are going, it will work for us.

You might say, "Even when I do start, I soon stop. Starting doesn't seem to get me anywhere." In fact, when you stop, you are once again "faced with a difficult task." And the counsel is still the same, *"Start!"* You may start as often as necessary. You must start as often as necessary for you to do what you want to do—to feel strong, to be effective.

When you have started, listen to the guidance available to you. You are like the ship under way, with your rudder to help

. . . when you let it

with any potential difficulty. Be responsive to the guidance that comes silently to you. The more you allow yourself to be guided by these inner messages, the more you will receive.

A Metaphor for Life

The computer solitaire game of Free Cell is a beautiful illustration of what we gain when we operate out of an understanding that if we are stuck, we can start again. All the cards are "dealt" face up in eight columns on the computer screen. Above the columns are four empty spaces (free cells) to be used by you for temporary storage of cards that are in the way of a move you'd like to make. Four additional empty spaces are at the top. The object of the game is to put all the cards of one suit, starting with Ace and ending with King, on each of these four spaces. Like regular solitaire, you can be stuck, either because you can't figure out any move or a message appears on the screen: "Sorry, you lose. There are no more legal moves." Unlike regular solitaire, when you see that message, you have the option to play again with the exact same "deal" using a different strategy. The computer has stored the deal for just this purpose; that's the special feature of the computer version of the game. To play again, all you need to do is click on "Restart."

Apparently, *every deal can be won* eventually. So we have this metaphor for life: If you are stuck for any reason, you can start again, as many times as you like. And each trial is a learning experience. You can notice what did not work and try something different next time, maybe slightly different or totally different. If after a few moves, you see that what you're doing is not working, you can click on Restart; you don't have to wait until you receive the "Sorry, you lose" message. You can learn from your mistakes, start over, and win.

In Free Cell, managing the Aces and Kings is important. You have to get the Aces out quickly and create empty columns for the Kings. When you look at a new deal, you see where those key cards are and set out to take advantage of their locations or overcome them. You don't like to see them buried under five or six other cards but, if they are, you can manage them. And you win. Or you click on Restart and win the next time.

Why is life not that easy? In Free Cell, we have two major advantages. One is that when we look at the "deal," we are likely to just look at what is. We won't be wondering why we were given this deal, who gave us this deal, or what's wrong with us that we were given this deal. Instead, we'll just look at where the Aces and Kings are, what moves are available to us, and which ones might be better. The second advantage is that we will learn as we go: we can always click on Restart, and we will win! We're either learning or winning. And we're not just learning how to win with the deal we're working on; we're learning how to win, how to succeed in general.

The Restart option is available to us every day, and we can help ourselves by operating out of that principle. This means, when faced with a difficult task, do what J. Krishnamurti taught: just look at what is, without interpretation, judgment, fear, or a label. Look at what actions are available and which ones might be better. Know that you will either succeed or learn, your learning will help you with the next difficult task, and ultimately you'll win.

YOU DON'T NEED TO KNOW THE ANSWER

At the outset, when faced with a difficult task, you may not know how you'll win. The outworking of your life may be quite different from what you were thinking initially. When I moved to Roanoke, Virginia, I thought I was going there for a job, a new career, but four years later the job disappeared when the world price of oil collapsed. By that time, however, I was happily married to Sharon, who would play an important role in my life in general and my spiritual development in particular. When Sharon moved to Roanoke, she thought she was going to take care of her father, who was terminally ill. Three years later, her father passed away, and a year after that she was happily married, too.

. . . when you let it

Another example of how our lives unfold for the best after we start involves a young man I know who was headed for college, thinking of majoring in business. His father, a successful businessman, advised him to study something he really liked because he would have plenty of time for business later. The young man went to an outstanding university and graduated with a degree in sculpture. At that point, he was faced with the difficult task of finding work. He found no opportunities for someone with his credentials. He liked boats and found a job helping to build boats in a boatyard. (Start!) Later he got to know a boatyard customer, a successful executive, who talked with him, told him he should be in finance, and subsequently offered him a job, which he accepted. The young man saw that he was good at his new job and decided to go to graduate school to pursue an MBA. He wanted only the best for himself, so he applied to what he thought was the best school in the country and was accepted. After he graduated, he created an outstanding career for himself. When he took the job in the boatyard, he started on his career, even though at the time he did not yet know what his career would be.

GETTING STARTED

When you have a difficult task at hand, allow yourself to slow down and listen; you hear *"Start!"* and you start. Soon, you feel heavy and hear another voice saying, "This will never work," Or, "Why are you doing this to yourself?" or other negative ideas. You stop. You're now faced with the same difficult task as before. Allow yourself to again hear the word *"Start!"* See *Start!* as your ticket to a different way of being; start again. You make some progress and stop again. *Start!*

See that you don't have to be limited by the tasks before you. You're okay and you can move forward. Every time you stop, start again. Keep doing this until you're done. And be aware of what happens inside you when letting go of your resistance to difficult tasks. See that you have more strength, maybe more courage.

everything turns out right . . .

Welcome opportunities to do difficult tasks. They are our teachers. They come to us to remind us of what we can do to liberate ourselves from old beliefs in our limitations. What's the pay-off? *The growth and strength that come from choosing to do a difficult task easily.* In most cases, we become aware that at any time we can choose not to do it. Rob can pay someone to paint his house. Jim can find another job. Dan, Diane, and Rachel can find someone else to break the news. Rebecca, on the other hand, will not refuse to pick up the children. She will not make them suffer from her conflict with others who are not doing their share. She will deal with the other parents later.

When you accept the situation, the pain eases. Recognizing that you have a choice, consciously exercising that choice, and doing or not doing the "difficult" task because you want to, frees you up to do the job without resistance, or not do it at all. The key is to *Start!*

When you are consistently practicing *Start!,* notice that you have fewer difficult tasks, and they don't seem so difficult. The assortment of tasks hasn't changed—you have. In due time, you will reach the point where you know that when you start any job, you'll either complete it and have more fun in the process, or you'll learn. In either case, you will fill your life with more confidence, energy, and love.

. . . when you let it

Summary

◇   When faced with a difficult task, *Start!*

◇   Let go of your resistance.

◇   If necessary, start again.

◇   Like a ship's rudder, your guidance needs you to be moving in order to work.

◇   Welcome difficult tasks. They are your teachers.

◇   *Start!* is your ticket to a different way of being.

4

Just when You Think You've Run out of Time, You're Done

*"For everything there is a season
and a time for every matter under heaven."*
—Ecclesiastes 3:1

It's a perception, a point of view. Running out of time sounds a lot like failure, while "you're done" sounds like success. If you think you've "run out of time," you're making a negative judgment about yourself, as if something bad has happened. You're comparing your performance with a plan, a concept. Let's shift the perception. Before we do that, let's look at what's going on when you think you've run out of time.

YOU HAVE NOT RUN OUT OF TIME

Some alternative descriptions of what happens when we think we've run out of time are:

1. Your tasks were unfamiliar and you expected to finish them more quickly, so the results did not fit *your expectations*.

2. Some unexpected things happened that prevented you from doing what you *planned*.

3. Your boss, co-workers, management, friends, or relatives put *their expectations* on you and their expectations were unreasonable.

4. You're always late, that's just the way you are.

5. You didn't start in time.

6. You didn't start.

REQUIREMENTS

You are not *required* to do more than you did. Look at the alternatives again:

1. Meeting your expectations is not a requirement. You may think it's a requirement, but it may be just a way of supporting your self-image. A self-image that requires you to do something you don't know how to do is working against experiencing peace, joy, love, and compassion.

   The truth is, you needed to learn how to do the unfamiliar tasks before you could actually do them. In all kinds of business—manufacturing, distribution, sales, service—insufficient knowledge and training are major sources of delays. And oftentimes we don't know that we don't know how to do something until we're performing the task. That will cause delays.

2. Lack of knowledge can affect a family's plan, too. Last year, my grandchildren, Sharon, and I went to the Florida State Fair for the first time. We followed the driving directions we were given and became stalled in stop-and-go traffic for an hour outside the fairgrounds. We didn't know the quickest way to get there. We didn't know that the person giving us the directions didn't know the quickest way to get there when a State Fair is going on.

   Unexpected happenings are likely to prevent you from doing what you *planned*. But that's all. "Planned" is not the same as "required." The requirements in life are very few: keep your word, do to others as you would have them do to you, and extend love. The rest is what we elect to do, and don't *have* to.

3. The expectations of your boss, co-workers, management, friends, or relatives are only that. Not meeting their expectations may precipitate disappointment, frustration, or even anger among those whose expectations you are not meeting, but that is about them and their perceptions, not you. Maybe not meeting their expectations will lead to consequences: criticism, perhaps bitter criticism from those who feel threatened by the fact that you did not do more; an unwanted reassignment; loss of a job. Instead of focusing on that, you can focus on what you did, without attempting to convince the others that you deserve their approval. You are not required to do more than you did.

4. If you say, "I'm always late, that's just the way I am," you're agreeing to a deadline which you plan not to meet. You are declaring that you are not required to meet the deadline.

5. You didn't start on time, and 6. You didn't start at all, are discussed in Chapter 3.

LEARNING

What are you supposed to be learning from events such as these? You've had the experience of not doing what you planned to do. Nevertheless, when the deadline came, you were done.

1. One of the things you can learn from results that do not fit your *expectations* is this: you can change your expectations. Your expectations of yourself are not grounded in reality, just an out-picturing of who you want to be or who you think you're supposed to be. So if you find yourself "running out of time," change your expectations. Let your self-image support you experiencing peace, joy, love, and compassion.

everything turns out right . . .

The Florida State Fair episode provided a great opportunity to share with the five- and ten-year-old grandchildren the critical question: What are we to learn from this? As we approached the fairgrounds, we saw a much better way to go. And we decided that next year we would go early because the fair offered a lot to see and do.

2. The unexpected teaches that you don't have control over everything that happens and that's okay. Only the *fulfillment* of the plan is incomplete. You're okay. You're still the same wonderful person you've always been. And if you were to attempt to anticipate every possible unexpected happening, you would be much less productive, spontaneous, and creative. You would not be in the flow.

3. What are you to learn from the lofty or unreasonable expectations of your family, friends, co-workers, bosses, or management? First, you need to identify them as lofty or unreasonable. You want to avoid being flattered into thinking that you can do it all—unless you know that you *can* do it all and *want* to do it all. Second, you need to reject these expectations for yourself. Notice that this is about *you* fulfilling expectations of *others*, of the people in your life. You need first to learn to establish your own expectations and then explore with the others how your expectations can be merged with theirs.

4. The person who says, "I'm always late, that's just the way I am" is only partially right. " . . . always late" may be accurate, unless that person takes pride in being late and is exaggerating. But, "That's just the way I am," is not true. Being late is a choice. What can be learned from being late because that's just the way you are? The question is not, "Why are you late?" (The answer is that you are always doing something else that you prefer.) The question is, "Why do you choose to be late?"

What's the payoff for being late? Do you have a sense of being in control? Are you resisting authority (the authority of the clock or the person who sets the deadlines)? Are you saying, "You can't make me do it"? Do you think it gives you "more time"? (You can't get "more time.") Do you thrive on the pressure that accompanies being late? Once you realize that always being late is a choice, you can learn what is behind it. You can learn something important about what motivates you, and you can make a better choice *for yourself.*

Shifting Our Perceptions: First Stage

As you begin to shift your perceptions from running out of time to being done, you will benefit from having contingency plans.

Everyday Situations

Suppose you are busy in the late afternoon and early evening— doing chores, picking up the children from their after-school activities, grocery shopping, preparing dinner. You have a household guideline: serve dinner by 6:00 p.m. so that the children can go to bed on time. You're doing all these things, and some of them take much longer than planned. You think you've run out of time, but you're done—done with the errands; you did as much as you had time for. At that point you decide not to prepare the dinner you planned. Now what will you do for dinner? Heat up canned spaghetti? Heat frozen dinners in the microwave? Get Chinese takeout? Have pizza delivered? Fast food? Peanut butter and jelly sandwiches?

Is this the first time this has happened? If so, you are probably unprepared and you have a great learning opportunity. What will you learn? Maybe you'll have dinner at 6:30, everything will go well, and you'll learn that it's okay not to have dinner by 6:00 every night. An occasional "late dinner" will be fine. Or you learn that you can help the children go to bed promptly if you stock the ingredients for a fast, easy dinner in the future. Whatever the outcome, you will want to own the situation in which your original plan doesn't work out. When you accept the possibility of occasions when you won't be doing what you want to do, you will make a contingency plan.

If this has happened before, you have ingredients on hand for a quick dinner and can easily prepare the meal. As you prepare this quick dinner, you will be doing exactly what you *planned.* You will be happy with the outcome. *You're done* with the errands you're going to run before dinner and now you're going to prepare dinner. You get a little break. You didn't run out of time, you just reached the point where you realized you wanted to change plans. You're happy because dinner will be easier and a little different. If your contingency plan includes items you don't normally serve that the family likes, everyone will be happy.

If on previous occasions you've had the experience of not having enough time to prepare the kind of dinner you'd like, and you don't have on hand the makings of a quick dinner—i.e., no contingency plan—you may be resisting the idea that you will not always prepare the dinner you *plan.* To have a contingency plan would mean giving in to future circumstances, admitting that we will not always succeed in doing what we want. We want to be in control.

This discussion is not about running errands, preparing dinner, and the children going to bed on time. In some families, none of these is an issue. It is about the ways we perceive ourselves "running out of time." Perfectionism and the desire to control are twin attributes preventing us from seeing the way things are. We're afraid of running out of time. We don't want to contemplate "failure" because that would mean that *we* are failures, or that we are no good. In this scenario, most of what we do has a hidden agenda: we are proving ourselves over and over again. To whom? Superficially, at least, to ourselves. Less superficially, to authority, perhaps our inner parent, or to God. When we think we've run out of time, we're buying into this hidden agenda. We're saying that we didn't succeed, there's something wrong, and we are at fault. And we can look at this situation differently.

. . . when you let it

You can feel the comfort of knowing you are done (with picking up the children from their activities, picking up the dry cleaning, putting gas in the car, etc.) no matter how many things are left on your "to do" list. For one reason or other, or for several reasons, you have to stop what you're doing and move on to the main event—preparing dinner. You will help if you don't judge yourself.

A Learning Opportunity

Just when you think you've run out of time . . . is a learning opportunity. Each time you have feelings of frustration because you're "running out of time," remind yourself that you will soon be done. And what you have accomplished, or not accomplished, is okay. You were not born to complete tasks. When a task is not complete and you must move onto something else, close your eyes and listen to the voice that says, "You're done."

Exercise: Changing Your Perception

Think of a time when you were expected to do something that you didn't finish or didn't do. Take a deep breath, slowly exhale and listen to your expectations. Let go of others' expectations. Once again, listen to "You're done." Savor the moment. Let go. This is a divine moment. This is where you let go of who-you-thought-you-were and experience yourself as whole, complete, and perfect. You're done. Each time you have that feeling of frustration or disappointment around your perception of running out of time, do this. Listen to the inner voice that says, "You're done." Keep doing this until this principle is part of your inner knowing.

I have learned to do this through business travel. Before going on a business trip, I always have preparations to make, sometimes intense preparations. Upon sinking into my seat on the plane, I have that feeling of letting go, knowing I'm done. This does not mean that I did everything I had planned, or someone expected; I'm just done. On rare occasions, I will think of something else that I would like to have brought with me, so I will call home or the office and ask for the material to be sent to me. And I'm still done. This experience, repeated dozens of times, has taught me this principle.

Moving one step further, sometime you will arrive at the point when you simply do not finish some item that "had to be done." "Had to be done" is in quotes because the very fact that you did not do it shows that you didn't have to. You'll know that you did as much as you could and now you are ready to ask the question, "What am I supposed to learn from this?"

Your issue may be commitment vs. over-commitment. Commitment is wonderful; over-commitment saps our strength. Or the issue is one of the six described at the beginning of the chapter. As you reflect on it, you will know. And you stand to benefit, perhaps in ways you cannot foresee, when you discover what you can learn from this experience.

Major Events

When we prepare for a major event, we will reach a point when "Time's up!" "The show must go on!" Sometimes literally. I've been part of a church men's group hosting a pancake breakfast starting at 8:30 on Sunday morning. When the day came, we scurried around making preparations. When the clock showed 8:30, we might have thought that we'd run out of time for this pancake breakfast but, as a matter of fact, we were done. Except for cooking the pancakes, the preparations were complete and we served breakfast. We didn't run out of time. We did what we could do and the pancake breakfast began. Not because the group did everything we wanted to do, but because we did what we had to do and at 8:30 we opened the doors. If we hadn't done what we had to do, we would have apologized to everyone for any inconvenience and canceled the breakfast. Then we would ask ourselves, "What are we supposed to be learning from this?"

. . . when you let it

This is a model for all "running out of time" scenarios. We work diligently to prepare for the major event. The plan is comprehensive, perhaps geared to be the best ever. We do not do everything in the plan and, when the time comes for the event to start, we're done. We can derive a lot of satisfaction from all that we and our friends, relatives, co-workers, bosses, and management did. If we don't do everything that we *had* to do, we postpone or cancel the event. Postponement or cancellation is okay. We can learn from all of this.

ANOTHER MAJOR EVENT—DEATH

I once gave a talk to a church group on the subject of death. My view was that we all will go through the process sooner or later, and, if we practice ahead of time, when the time comes, we can do well. I led the audience in the process of experiencing our own deaths. To help people get comfortable with the idea of practicing death, I offered the following poem I had written:

Death and I
Death and I walk hand in hand,
not as a jailer and a prisoner do
with handcuffs forming a wall between,
but more like a mother and child:
the mother guiding with sympathy and wisdom,
the child maturing with wonder and respect.

I recognized death as a constant companion and made it okay. It is. I was becoming aware that even death turns out right . . . when you let it.

To understand that death is part of life is the first step towards having a contingency plan. After that, when the time comes that we realize we can't do what we plan (i.e., live forever), we'll have a context for a contingency plan. That time could be today or off in the distant future. The moment of our death may be totally unforeseen or may be preceded by months of a terminal illness. In either case, we want that moment of death to be accompanied by the message, "You're done," signifying completion.

To reach that point requires a shift in everyday thinking from "I've run out of time" to "I'm done." Here the emphasis is on the everyday thinking—letting go of the habit of perceiving oneself as running out of time and into the habit of perceiving oneself "done."

Some of the elements of a contingency plan might be to express love and appreciation to the people you care about. You may want to ask them for forgiveness or extend forgiveness to them. You will want to fulfill any promises or commitments to them. These people will include immediate family, extended family, friends, co-workers, bosses, and others you are close to. When you are comfortable with that, you can widen your scope to include many acquaintances, neighbors, people you meet in stores, drivers on the road with you, teammates, fellow volunteers at churches and civic organizations, everyone. You may want to do something to express that love and appreciation. You may want to do these things now.

This discussion is about us dying. But we will probably experience the death of someone else before we pass on ourselves. We don't want to run out of time with them, either. We want our relationships to be complete when the time comes. What does it take to have a complete relationship, one with no unfinished business? The same as for our own passing: expressions of love and appreciation to the people we care about as well as forgiveness from them or to them. And we will want to fulfill any promises or commitments to them. Then when that person passes on, our grief and sadness will not be tinged with guilt and remorse. We will be done.

SHIFTING OUR PERCEPTIONS: SECOND STAGE

The second stage of shifting our perceptions moves beyond contingency plans.

. . . when you let it

LIVING IN THE MOMENT

The second stage is not thinking of running out of time or being done. At this stage, you know that everything is in Divine Order. You know what to do, and you do whatever is appropriate. When you formulate and use contingency plans, you become accustomed to the experience of being done. By doing this repeatedly, you gain confidence in your ability to complete what you planned. That includes knowing that some tasks or series of tasks cannot be completed in the available time. In that case, you will develop a different plan before you start. From there, your planning and activities will enable you to accomplish whatever you set out to do. You will gradually move into a kind of timeless place, and you will always be on time. You will be living in the moment. *And the payoff is that each time you start something, you will know that at the right time you will be done.*

Think about the first time and the last time you did a particular task with a deadline, such as completing your income tax return, giving a party, or writing a performance review. Was it much easier the last time than the first? Perhaps it took less clock time and less energy. Maybe it was not fun the first time and is now enjoyable. Perhaps you didn't meet the deadline the first time you tackled it and got done quickly the last time. Notice how much better the last time feels than the first did. This is the way you feel when you're living in the moment. You feel light. The task feels *do-able*.

GETTING THINGS DONE

What does it take to get things done? At the highest level of our endeavors, it takes loving, dedicated people with a dream, a plan, and courage to move forward in the direction of the dream. At every level, it takes understanding the goal, and having desire, commitment, and energy. That's what you bring to the process.

When the Second Stage shift in perception has taken place, the things you want to get done, that you expect to get done and have agreed to get done, will get done. You will move out of the "yes or no" realm of running out of time to being done, and your life will be complete at every moment.

How does all this fit with *everything turns out right . . . when you let it?* "You're done" conveys a sense of completion, that what we've worked on has turned out right.

SUMMARY

◈ Just when you think you've run out of time, you're done.

◈ It's a matter of perception; shift your perception.

◈ Form contingency plans.

◈ Establish your own expectations of yourself.

◈ When you live in the moment, you never run out of time.

5

If at First You Don't Succeed,
Relax and You Will

"As soon as you trust yourself, you will know how to live."
—Goethe

I was on a business trip in Dublin, Ireland, accompanied by Sharon. My host made reservations for dinner for the three of us and his wife. We were seated in the restaurant and had just been served drinks when all the lights went out. The power outage we had thought was a minor inconvenience proved to have shut down the kitchen and would require a visit from a power company repairman. Our host predicted a long delay, excused himself, and left. A short while later he returned beaming. He had gotten us a table at a nearby restaurant, *Rolly's*! It is so popular that reservations must be made weeks in advance, and we were the beneficiaries of a cancellation. Our host did not succeed at first, but relaxed and enabled us to have a grand evening at the restaurant that was his first choice.

This idea is quite different from the one I grew up with: "If at first you don't succeed, try, try, again." *Try* contains the idea of failure. For example, if I put a quarter in my hand and invite you to try to pick it up, as soon as you lift it off, you've actually picked up the quarter! You're no longer trying; you've done it. But if you *try* to pick up the quarter, the quarter doesn't come up, because you're only trying. In fact, you're doing nothing, with no movement; your fingers must be still in order to just try to pick it up.

This expression, "If at first you don't succeed (the first time you try), try, try again" says not to expect to succeed the first time you try. The second "try" says you may not succeed the second time either. And "try again" says clearly you may fail the third time. Nevertheless, you're going to keep trying, probably without succeeding, at least for a while. This old adage seems to be celebrating dogged determination instead of success.

RELAX AND YOU WILL

The corollary above says, . . . *relax and you will.* In the 1800s, Thomas Edison tried thousands of substances as possible filaments for the incandescent light bulb. Nikola Tesla, an Edison employee whose genius was off the scale and who later invented alternating current, looked on in amazement and reportedly muttered, "Just a moment of calm reflection would reveal the successful outcome." That is, " . . . relax and you will, Tom."

Closer to home, my daughter Laura, who is a computer programmer, recently told me about a job she had been doing that day. "While fixing someone's program, I'd gotten stuck and nothing I did worked. Then I took a break and a deep breath and said to myself, 'I *know* what the problem is,' although at the moment I had not yet realized what it was. At that point, I went back to the job and quickly saw the problem and the solution. I knew what the problem was before I was consciously aware of it. I knew that someplace inside, I had the answer. This enabled me to relax and succeed."

If we know that what we're doing is going to turn out right when we let it, we can relax and let it. This includes the idea that we will work diligently on the task at hand and without emotional attachment to the outcome.

Playing out of Your Mind

For about 10 years, I played squash regularly. This game is played on a court with four walls and a high ceiling that are all part of the playing area. The racquet is about the size of a badminton racquet and very sturdy. The ball is small, a little larger than a golf ball, and not very resilient. When you drop the ball from eye level to the floor, it only bounces up to knee level. Since it doesn't bounce much, you must be very quick to hit it before the second bounce and return it to the front wall without it touching the floor. And you must concentrate. Many times, I have concentrated so hard I was aware of only the ball, where I was on the court, and, dimly, where my opponent was. Sometimes I would slip into a kind of dream state, only aware of the ball. At that point, I was playing very well. My opponents and fellow players often had the same experience. We called this kind of performance "playing out of your mind."

W. Timothy Gallwey describes this phenomenon and also calls it "playing out of your mind."[6] The key characteristic, he writes, " . . . is what might be called 'mindlessness.' There seems to be an intuitive sense that the mind is transcended—or at least in part rendered inoperative. Athletes in most sports use similar phrases, and the best of them know that their peak performance never comes when they're thinking about it."

The superior play continues until the player becomes conscious of what he's doing and attempts to take control. Then he loses it. Notice that it is not a setback, the loss of a point perhaps, which breaks the spell. Becoming questioning, analytical, or judgmental takes us out of *the zone.*

The Bible gives us an example of this. Peter and other followers of Jesus were out in a boat at night on the Sea of Galilee. Jesus approached them, walking on the water. Peter called out to Jesus. He wanted him to tell Peter to come to him on the water. Jesus said, "Come." Peter proceeded to walk on the water towards Jesus. As he walked, the wind and waves rose and he

everything turns out right . . .

became frightened and began to sink. Jesus admonished him for being of little faith, saying, " . . . why did you doubt?"[7]

A similar case involves the fire walk, or the practice of walking on red-hot coals in bare feet. An acquaintance of mine attended a workshop in which all the attendees were prepared to fire walk. When his turn came, he started out all right but, after he had gone several feet, he looked down and started thinking about what he was doing. Immediately, the coals started to burn and he had to jump off.

An excellent illustration of this experience is the remarkable shot making by Michael Jordan, professional basketball superstar, in the first half of the first game of the 1992 National Basketball Association finals. He was playing extremely well, scoring 35 points before the end of the first half. (This is a lot of points for a whole game, let alone less than a half, and is still the record for a finals game.) After sinking a seemingly effortless long (three-point) shot to bring his total to 35, he ran back up the court to play defense. He was smiling with his arms stretched up and out, palms up, and slowly shaking his head as if to say, "This is great and I don't know how I'm doing it." For the rest of the game, he scored just two points. Up to the moment when he became self-conscious about his superlative play, he was "playing out of his mind," out of an inner knowing of what to do and how to do it. His self-awareness took him out of the zone he was in, and he never got back into it that night.

On April 8, 2001, Tiger Woods won the Masters Golf Tournament and became the first player ever to hold the four major golf titles in the world at the same time. The next day's St. Petersburg Times reported:

> *Woods cried on the 18th green Sunday. "I was in such a zone, working so hard on every shot," Woods said. "I walked over to the side and started thinking, 'I don't have any more shots to play. I'm done. I've won the Masters.' I started realizing what I had done."*

He had just done what seemed to be impossible—win four major tournaments in a row—and he was so deep into his zone

. . . when you let it

that he needed a few minutes to become consciously aware of the achievement. Being deep in the zone certainly contributed to his play and his championship.

Many of us have heard about couples who had trouble conceiving; they went to doctors and fertility specialists, followed all the advice, and still did not conceive. Then they adopted a baby or small child, and subsequently conceived.

Each of these illustrates a way of life. In squash, basketball and golf, or in walking on water or hot coals, the participants know what to do and do it, sometimes exceedingly well. In life, we know what to do, the knowledge comes from within us, and we need to let that inner knowing take over. Then we will do well. This is not to say that anyone can walk on water or score 35 points in one half of an NBA basketball game. However, when we let go of intense analysis of our situations and what we are doing, when we just let our lives unfold, we'll do well at what is ours to do.

Living Without Judgment

When we relax and live without judgment, without interpretation, without trying to understand why people are doing what they're doing, without resistance, and without questioning, we succeed. We're not disappointed. We're in the flow. We're lighter. We float. When we're floating, we succeed. Succeed in what? In whatever we want to do—in our relationships, in our parenting, in our jobs, in our personal growth, and in our interactions with friends, relatives, and strangers.

What is judgment anyway? Living without judgment is just looking at what is. Discernment is seeing that two things are different. Judgment is concluding that one thing is better than another. When we live with judgment, we're not relaxed, not succeeding.

How do we live without judgment? A place to start is to live without comparisons.

LIVING WITHOUT COMPARISONS

We hear many comparisons made by friends, co-workers, loved ones, and many others.

"It's not the best shrimp I've ever had."

"Did you see her shoes? I hate to say it but they may just be the ugliest I've ever seen."

"Winn-Dixie has much better beef than Kash N' Karry (or vice versa)."

"He's much (smarter/better looking/nicer) than his brother."

"These fireworks are much better than (not as good as) the ones we saw last year."

"This beach is not as good as (much better than) the one in Clearwater."

"We were supposed to take off an hour ago and we're still sitting here on the ground."

What do these comparisons have to do with relaxing and succeeding? Letting go of comparisons such as these are the baby steps we can take towards living without judgment. If we give up the practice of making comparisons, we won't be able to make judgments. Judgments are simply conclusions we draw from the comparisons we make. But we can more easily let go of comparisons regarding the fireworks and just enjoy what we're watching than we can let go of judging someone in our family who is wasting his life, spoiling her children, or living beyond his or her means. Letting go of comparisons is just a good place to start.

As illustrated above, we can make positive comparisons. Shall we let go of them, too? Yes. What's wrong with acknowledging that this is the best beach we've ever been to? Nothing, it just doesn't help us to relax and succeed. If we're living in the world of comparisons, we know that when we pick a new beach to visit, it could be more crowded, with a bigger drop-off (or a more gradual slope), with waves that are bigger or smaller, or not so clean as the one we're used to. These comparisons can slip into judgment ("This place is terrible!"). This possibility raises anxiety. So to cope with this anxious situation (of going to the beach!), we can read the guidebooks or read the newspaper clipping we saved for just this occasion: "Ten Best Beaches in the US," or, if we have more modest ambitions: "Ten Best Beaches in Our Metropolitan Area."

We can make our choice and hope, anxiously perhaps, the new beach is better. But what does success in going to the beach look like? Having fun with friends and family, swimming, splashing, watching the sun light up the water droplets, people-watching, picnicking, playing volleyball or Frisbee, building a castle, reading, listening to music, and/or relaxing? We can succeed at these on most beaches.

Clearly, this is not about beaches; it's about us. We can, and sometimes do, compare schools, churches, restaurants, stores, movies, friends, relatives, co-workers, and all the people who provide us with goods and services. And we can slip into judgment, reinforcing any negative feelings we have. Or we can relax and appreciate what unfolds.

LIVING WITHOUT INTERPRETATION

Interpretation is what we add to whatever we're observing in order to make the observations fit with our experience, knowledge, or bias. It's not what we're seeing or hearing. It's our attempt to fill in the gaps. It's our attempt to seem knowledgeable.

"Do you know what I think?" "I'll bet . . . " "Don't you see what he (or she) is doing?" Implying, "I can tell you." These are preludes to an interpretation.

Interpretation is born of the desire to figure things out. This is unnecessary. The more you try to figure things out, the more investment you will have in the outcome, and the farther away you will be from relaxation. You need only watch events unfold and help where you can.

To live without interpretation, you need only listen to yourself and make sure you are telling the simple truth, without adding anything, without modifying anything to fit a bias you may have. Just love the truth.

When you are accustomed to this practice, you may notice that others are eager to share their interpretations even when they are based on speculation. You may seek to dissuade them without success. Or you can relax and let go. And that will enable the others to relax too.

LIVING WITHOUT TRYING TO UNDERSTAND WHY PEOPLE ARE DOING WHAT THEY'RE DOING

From time to time, a friend or acquaintance will ask, "Why is he doing that?" referring perhaps to someone spending beyond his means. This is a way of saying, "I don't like what he is doing and I wish he would stop." This question has two difficulties. One is that if we ask the question of the person whose behavior we don't like, we won't receive the real answer because he doesn't know. The second difficulty is that, if we receive his best spur-of-the-moment answer, we won't like the answer any better than the behavior. On the other hand, the real answer, perhaps connected to human frailty, will help us be aware that we are all connected. It might elicit our compassion and love. And we don't have to know the real answer in order to respond lovingly.

LIVING WITHOUT RESISTANCE

The opposite of just "Looking at what is" is resisting the way it is. When we resist, we use a lot more energy. When we embrace the way it is and what we are doing, a lot of joy bubbles up into our life. The EST training captured this idea with the advice, "Ride the horse in the direction it's going," bringing up the alternative image of riding the horse facing backwards. That's an awkward picture. When we resist what is, we're like someone doing just that. When we relax and get together with our horse (everyday life), we succeed.

. . . when you let it

Parents sometimes resist the way their children behave. They have difficulty in providing the guidance and upbringing they want to give their children because, at various times and places, the children resist. The parents resist the child's resistance. They want the child to want to follow their instructions and the child does not. In their actions, the parents are modeling resistance. The child will benefit from being taught to live without resistance. As a parent, how can you teach them? Accept the principle that *if at first you don't succeed, relax and you will.* Live out of that principle. See your child's resistance as your opportunity to teach the child not to resist. Look for ways not to overcome the child's resistance but to dissolve it in your love. See your child's resistance as a reminder to you to live without resistance.

My grandson and I have had a good relationship for many years. My wife and I have seen him and his younger sister many Sunday afternoons. One day when he was nine, we were all playing in the swimming pool in our backyard. The time came for him to give a pool toy to his sister. He knew it was time to give it up, and he resisted. I insisted. He resisted. I insisted. He asked, "What will you do if I don't give it to her?"

I quietly told him, "You have no choice. You have to give her the toy." He proposed punishments for himself to be administered for not giving up the toy. I declined to set one. All this time, he was about 15 feet away, and I was not threatening him in any way. Finally, he threw the toy in my direction. I thanked him and explained, "It would have been better if you had handed it to your sister but it's okay." I thanked him again. When he left for the day, I gave him a hug and told him I enjoyed seeing him. He hugged back. It is now three years later and we have not had anything like that kind of standoff again. We are relating to each other without resistance, with love.

A business associate of mine was an independent industrial developer. I helped him with advice and some legwork as part of my job as director at the Science and Technology Center of Southern West Virginia. Much of his effort involved contacting people with a lot of responsibilities: plant managers, bankers, mayors, councilmen, and other industrial developers. My business associate was constantly frustrated by the fact that many of these people would be very slow to call him back and some of them did not return his calls at all. Many of them were slow to agree to a meeting date. My explanation—that these were busy people who had difficulty taking the time to return calls from members of their own organization and even more difficulty meeting with them—did not affect him. He chose to resist the way it was. He was not being called back and not meeting with these people when he wanted to. He was stressed and often angry when he told me of his frequent experiences of not having his calls returned. He did not discover the joy that relaxation brings, and he did not succeed.

I lived in Japan for nine months on a small army post in a small town. We were instructed in Japanese customs and culture, and had ample opportunity to observe them firsthand. I learned that Japan has had many natural disasters: earthquakes, typhoons, tidal waves, and volcanic eruptions. When talking about these events, Japanese people use the expression *Shikata ganai,* which translates to, "It cannot be helped." When applied to everyday life, it becomes a motto for living without resistance.

I have encountered resistance in my professional life on many occasions. Some of the signs I've seen are clear: arms folded across the chest, legs crossed, body turned away, no eye contact, and hunched up shoulders. My response must be to have this experience without resisting the behavior I see. I usually have to drop my shoulders, be ready to make eye contact, and turn off whatever signals I am sending out that come from my resistance. It is not a façade; I'm letting go from inside out. When I relax, I succeed because the people I am working with relax and succeed too. It may take a while, but it happens.

. . . when you let it

LIVING WITHOUT QUESTIONING

Why don't they . . .? How could they . . .? When will they stop
. . .? Why can't they . . .? Why do they . . .? What gives them the
right to . . .? I don't understand why . . .? Whenever we hear ourselves asking any of these questions or others like them, the time
has come for us to stop and quiet our minds. We need to let go
of the anxiety behind the question and listen to our inner guidance. Listen for guidance telling you to make the situation okay
or how you can help resolve it. Be quiet so you can hear your
inner voice. Listen for the voice that quietly says, "Relax, everything is okay."

WE SUCCEED

We're either succeeding or learning. The tasks may or may not
be done in the way or in the time we want, or at all. The issues
may or may not be resolved to our satisfaction. If they aren't,
we'll learn more about how to obtain satisfaction. When we give
up our judgments, trying to figure things out, trying to understand why people are doing what they're doing, resisting, and
questioning, then we will succeed even if all the tasks are not
done or the issues are not resolved in our favor.

What does lack of success feel like? Frustrating and dissatis-
fying. What does success feel like? Like we're "in the zone."
We're having experiences of love, peace and joy. We feel as if
everything is okay. (It is.) What does success look like?
Seemingly effortless demonstrations and expressions of love,
peace and joy.

One way to experience being in the flow is to walk a
labyrinth slowly in a meditative state. As you gently place one
foot in front of the other, you will be *guided* along your path
towards the labyrinth's center, your center. You're going to the
center although you don't know exactly how. You will frequently be led to change your direction while always on the path to
the center. It is a wonderful way to open yourself to guidance,

everything turns out right . . .

in this case provided by the labyrinth. This is the way life is: the more you relax, trust your guidance, and focus on your path, the more certain you are of success.

The labyrinth also provides another perspective on life. When you look from a short distance at a labyrinth with many people walking it, you'll see them all going in different directions. It looks chaotic. If you didn't know labyrinths, it would be hard to understand what is going on. You realize, however, that all of them are on their own paths and by following their guidance, they all will reach their goals. That's the way life, your life, works.

Summary

◈ If at first you don't succeed, relax and you will.

◈ When you know everything turns out right, you will relax more easily and let your life unfold.

◈ Allow yourself to be in the flow by reacting to every situation effortlessly.

◈ Relaxing includes working diligently on the task at hand.

◈ Have no emotional attachment to the outcome.

◈ Live without making comparisons or judgments.

◈ Live without trying to figure things out, without trying to understand why people are doing what they're doing, without interpretation, without resistance, and without questioning.

. . . when you let it

trying
doing,
ithout

6

You Are the Person You'd Like to Become

"This above all: to thine own self be true."
—Shakespeare

The fact that you are reading this book indicates that you might like to see the world differently. You might like to shift your assumptions concerning how the world works from Murphy's Law, *Anything that can go wrong, will* to Charlie's Law™, *Everything turns out right . . . when you let it.* Or from, "The world is a hostile place" to "The world is a friendly place." Or from, "Work is competitive" to "Work is cooperative." Or from "We live in a world of scarcity" to "We live in a world of plenty."

In *Conversations with God*, God is talking about going to heaven and says, "Enlightenment is understanding that there is nowhere to go, nothing to do, and nobody you have to be except exactly who you're being right now."[8] So, there is nobody else you have to be.

In *A Course in Miracles* the Voice tells us, "When peace comes at last to those who wrestle with temptation and fight against the giving in to sin; when the light at last comes into the mind given to contemplation; or when the goal is finally achieved by anyone, it always comes with just one happy realization; *'I need do nothing.'*[9]

In *THIS IS IT*, Alan Watts describes "the Buddhist realization that . . . the enlightenment or awakening is not the creation of a new state of affairs but the recognition of what always is."[10]

So we have the same message from God, the Voice for God, and the Buddha: *we need do nothing*. Okay, but how are we going to go from here (the person we are now) to there (the person we'd like to become) if we don't do anything? We have a desire to change and we're advised that we don't need to do anything. A Buddhist principle teaches us the practice of doing without doing. John Bradshaw has taught us the value of changing from a human doing to a human being. And an effective path of self-development is: be, do, have. This chapter focuses on being.

BE, DO, HAVE

The conventional approach to personal development is have, do, be: have a dance costume, dance, and then, in time, become a dancer. A child can have a baseball uniform, play baseball, and, in time, become a baseball player. On the other hand, if the child follows the path of be, do, have, he or she will become a dancer or a ballplayer just by being one.

The concept of "be, do, have" is illustrated by a boy learning to ride a bike. Our minister tells of his young son coming to him saying he wanted a bike. (In his mind, he was *being* a bike rider.) His father told him that when he could ride a bike, he would be given one. He suggested to his son that he learn on his friend's bike. So the boy did and later demonstrated to his father he could ride it. He was *doing* what bike riders do. Then his father bought him his own bike. At that point, he *had* a bike.

This is in contrast to the way my children learned to ride their bikes. First they were given bikes; they had their bikes. Next they learned to ride them; they were doing bike-riding. Finally, when they were skilled at it, they *were* bike riders. This is not as powerful as the first method.

EXERCISE: BE THE PERSON YOU'D LIKE TO BECOME

The idea is that the place to start experiencing yourself as the person you would like to become is to *be* that person. Then allow the process of becoming to unfold. If you'd like to be more loving, more compassionate, more generous, or more of anything that fits the person you'd like to become, experience yourself that way, right now. To start, read the next paragraph and then practice the exercise it contains.

Close your eyes and think of a very pleasant personal experience you have had. It might be sitting on a beautiful beach, looking at a mountain panorama, giving or receiving a kiss, giving or receiving a very special gift, flying in a small plane, soaring in a hot air balloon, seeing your newborn for the first time. Feel those feelings. Stay with them. If you lose them, reconnect with the image and re-experience the feelings. Allow them to grow. Allow them to overwhelm you. Float in them. Feel them. That's you. Start now and when you are done, come back to this page.

EXERCISE: BEING LOVING

Now do this again and add feelings of love, extending love to someone you care about. You might be with a loved one who is sharing the experience or the feelings of love with you. Or you might be alone filled with wonderful, indescribable, loving sensations. This is also you. Is this the way you want to live your life? (Say "Yes.") It's available to you.

EXPERIENCING YOURSELF AS THE PERSON YOU'D LIKE TO BECOME

Can you expect to experience yourself as the person you'd like to become when you finish this chapter? No, the process is going to take time. You could ask, "If I'm not going to *do* anything, why will experiencing myself differently take time?" Because you're not yet accustomed to meeting all of the challenges of

everything turns out right . . .

everyday life with love, compassion, generosity, humility, for-giveness, and all the other responses the person you'd like to become would make. How can you go from here to there?

In the course of a day, week, or month, you experience a range of emotions. The longer the period you look at, the greater will be the range of emotions. That is, once in a great while, you will have a high high, and also once in a great while, you'll have a low low. In between, you'll have ups and downs. What follows is a way to shift your self-awareness. As you proceed with this, let your inner voice help you identify and reinforce the feelings that come up.

Every time you are up, having a high, or a high high (with-out any alcohol or drugs, just from the pleasure of the moment) be aware that *this is who you are!* Own the feelings and know you can live with these feelings more and more. When the feelings of well being, of being the person you want to be, start to fade, allow them to slip away. They'll come back.

Every time you are down, having a low, or a low low (with-out any alcohol or drugs, just from the pressure of the moment) be aware that *this is also who you are!* Own the feelings. Just look at the circumstances of this low without judgment. Realize that these feelings are not a part of the person you'd like to become. Gently let go of them. They are part of you but you are losing them; you are giving up a part of yourself; you are moving toward a new self, a new self-image. This letting go is a signifi-cant shift. It may not seem like much at first, but repeated many times—every time you are down, low, or at a low low—the shift will be more and more apparent, more a part of who you are.

OWNING WHO YOU ARE

Why would you want to own the feelings of being down? Not owning them results in living without acknowledging them or, to put it another way, by operating on top of them. What's wrong with that? Those feelings will always be within us, emerg-ing over and over again, despite our pushing them away. Each

. . . when you let it

time something happens that we don't like, those feelings will pop up. Don't we often react that way? In other words, something happens that we don't like and we become down, upset, or angry. Isn't that how life is? No. It doesn't have to be that way. That's not the reaction of the person you'd like to become. You would prefer to be loving, compassionate, forgiving in all circumstances. That's available.

On tennis, squash, and racquetball courts and golf courses, I have seen players become frustrated and angry with themselves. On one such occasion, the player threw his golf club high in the air and it landed in a virtually inaccessible spot in a bramble bush, heightening his frustration. In acting as if their poor play is not a normal part of their game, these players are deceiving themselves. Until they own their error-prone play—acknowledge that they do play that way—they will have difficulty improving their golf scores. In other words, you can't change what you don't own.

One of my most disappointing teaching experiences came to me as a graduate assistant coaching (tutoring) a chemical engineering student in his junior year. He was receiving poor grades and I encouraged him to see me during my office hours to get my help. He came in several times but I was unable to help him in any substantial way. As soon as I started an explanation, he would interrupt and exclaim that he got it. He did this almost every time. He didn't learn anything from me because he never acknowledged that he needed to learn.

So, the idea is to hold on to the best and let go of the rest. This is not like the song in *A Chorus Line* in which one of the aspiring dancers sings, "Keep the best of you, do (fix) the rest of you." Letting go is different from fixing. Recognize this: you already *are* the person you'd like to become, and these feelings of being out of sorts are not a part of that person. Know that anytime you're feeling down, angry, low, upset, low low, frustrated—that is, unlike the person you'd like to become—you can find the source of those feelings within yourself.

everything turns out right . . .

FINDING THE SOURCE OF UNWANTED FEELINGS AND LETTING THEM GO

To find the source of negative or unloving feelings, I have asked myself when was the first time I could remember feeling that way. Next, when I found the answer to the question, I realized that those circumstances were gone and could no longer hurt me. As a result, I found it easy to stand back from that long ago event and let go of the feelings arising from it. The last step was to let go of the feelings of being down, angry, low, etc. in my present situation. I did this by recognizing that I was carrying those feelings around from long ago, waiting for something to let me give them expression. I'd tell myself I didn't need to react that way. Although I had not yet learned that I am the person I'd like to become, I wanted to let go of those feelings.

For me, one of the triggers was the time when I was about 9 years old and a boy I often played with beat me up. Looking back as an adult, I saw that he could no longer hurt me and I forgave him. Then the negative feelings in me as an adult— resentment and victimhood—melted.

On another occasion, I was driving to work over a narrow, hilly road, thinking about something that had happened in which I felt somewhat betrayed. I was 56 years old at the time, and I flashed back to when I was about 10. I remembered my mother hitting me with the back of her hairbrush, something she had often threatened but never done. On that day, she had broken our tacit agreement: I would misbehave and aggravate her, she would threaten to "take the brush to me," and I would stop just short of her breaking point. This time, I had miscalculated. Driving to work and thinking about the past event, I was overcome by my feelings and started to sob. Unable to see to drive, I forced myself to stop crying and told myself that I could get in touch with those feelings later. As if to reassure myself that I could recapture those feelings, I allowed myself to re-experience the childhood event and immediately started sobbing again, unable to see well enough to drive. I regained my compo-

. . . when you let it

sure once more and drove to work. Later, I thought about the childhood event from time to time, but without experiencing it again. As a result of this, I let go of feelings of betrayal. The adult experience in which I felt somewhat betrayed was just what I needed, both to let go of those feelings and to learn how to let go of other negative feelings.

Once was usually not enough. Often after letting go of the negative feelings, they would re-appear. As soon as I was aware of them, I would repeat the process of recalling the earliest experience of those feelings, knowing I could no longer be hurt by what happened long ago, and letting go of the hurt and the feelings I had. Each time the negative feelings re-appeared in response to what was going on in my life at the time, they were less intense. During many cycles of this process, the feelings became less and less intense and finally virtually disappeared entirely. They still come up occasionally, less and less frequently, and I am helped in this process by the knowledge that I am the person I'd like to become. I can let them go.

You can do more than I did. I could have helped myself enormously by replacing with forgiveness whatever negative feelings came up. The negative feelings were invariably due to something done by someone else or me (real or imagined). If I had forgiven that someone or myself, I would have let go much more quickly. You can practice forgiveness every time you feel the negative feelings, either in your current episode of discomfort or the one you are recalling from your past. You can forgive the person who *seems* to be causing you discomfort, knowing you can find the source within yourself.

Nothing in this process suggests accepting abuse. In any abusive situation, removing yourself from the situation to a place of physical and emotional safety is of paramount importance. Once there, you will have time to look at the perpetrator with forgiveness and compassion. This may take a lot of time— weeks, months, years. Whenever the negative feelings—fear, anger, rage, etc.—come up, recognize that they are not part of the person you'd like to become, and let them go again, remembering: "If at first you don't succeed, relax and you will." Each time negative feelings come up, you will be a little stronger and able to experience yourself as the person you'd like to become, albeit briefly.

The following fairy tale illustrates a process bringing us closer and closer to the core of our being.

A SWEDISH FAIRY TALE

Once upon a time, a king and queen had a beautiful daughter. When it was time for the girl to be married, her parents told her she had to marry the dragon that was marauding through their kingdom. Marriage to her was the only thing that would appease the dragon and bring peace to the kingdom. Now the dragon was a fierce, ugly creature, covered with scales, and with horns, fangs, and sharp claws. The princess was deeply afraid of him, as was everyone in the kingdom. She cried and protested, but her parents were adamant. They told her to go to the fairy witch in the village, who would surely help her.

The fairy witch told her that on her wedding night she was to wear ten petticoats and dresses, one on top of the other. When she and the dragon arrived at the bridal chambers, she was to tell the groom that she was going to undress, and when she took off a dress, he had to take off one layer of his scaly hide. And that was what she did. He was so enchanted with his beautiful bride and her willingness to share his bed that he agreed. So, when she had taken off her outermost dress, he immediately began tearing off his scales in a terribly painful procedure. As soon as he had one layer off, she took off another dress and waited for him to take off another layer of scales. He did this, but only with great agony. As he pulled and pulled, he hurt terribly. Finally, he had another layer of scales off. When the princess took off another dress, the dragon once again tore off a layer of scales with much suffering. They continued this—one dress or petticoat after another followed by one layer of scales after another— until she had removed all of those garments and the dragon was removing his last layer of scales. Those last scales were softer and

. . . when you let it

more pliable than the others and came off easily, revealing a hand-some man. His skin was soft, his features were fine. Imagine the princess's delight and the dragon/man's relief! Having married in accordance with the wishes of the king and queen, they lived happily ever after.

This is how growth is for us. In order to experience ourselves as the person we'd like to become, we need to let go of our protective coating, our protective armor. The process doesn't have to be painful, although if you have lots of scales it will be. This fairy tale is an allegory for experiencing ourselves as the ones we would like to become by removing the barriers to that awareness. The more well known fairy tale of the ugly duckling tells us our self-perception can be way off the mark. The beautiful swan, you, grows up surrounded by ducks that look different and behave differently.

CHANGES, LOSS, GRIEVING

Experiencing yourself as the person you'd like to become primarily involves a lot of letting go. Letting go of what? Letting go of the undesirable, fearful, insecure parts of yourself that have been with you for many years. They may have been with you as long as you can remember. And now you're giving them up. You'll experience this loss the way we experience more familiar losses, such as the death of a relative or friend, the end of a relationship, the loss of a job either by layoff or resignation, or loss of community by moving to another place. Part of you is going to fade away.

In my own letting go process, the most difficult step was giving up my negative humor. Starting when I was a teenager and continuing for the next 40 years, being funny was one of the major aspects of my personality. People liked me because I was funny. I wrote skits performed at farewell dinners when I worked at the research center of a large oil company, and I was sought after for those events. Most of the humor was negative: teasing, put-downs, disparagements, distortions, and some insults.

This lasted until the summer of 1982, when my personal transformation was beginning. I had a wonderful relationship with a woman who did not like or accept my negative humor. In order to keep her respect, I had to stop, and I did. I still had negative thoughts and sometimes they reached the tip of my tongue, but they stopped there. Soon after that relationship ended, I met Sharon, the woman I married three years later, and she had the same distaste for my negative humor. So I continued to let go, gradually realizing that I was the person I'd like to become and that negative humor had no place in my life. How could I be a loving, compassionate person if I was making jokes at the expense of those around me? I decided I couldn't.

My awareness that negative humor was incompatible with the person I wanted to become was not sufficient to make the transition easy for me. For years I grieved the loss of the "negative humor" part of me. I wanted to be well liked, and humor was something I had used with great success. Now I couldn't do that anymore; I didn't know how to be humorous without being negative. I looked for ways to create positive humor with little success. Over the ensuing years, I have fully accepted my loss and have found some positive humor, which I certainly appreciate. My negative humor attracted friends who enjoyed that kind of humor. I lost many of them, too.

This experience illustrates the point that, as you recognize you are the person you'd like to become, you will have a sense of loss, perhaps a deep sense of loss. You could lose most of your friends and all of your acquaintances, just as if you were moving to a new job at a new location, whether by promotion or resignation. These are palpable losses even though the job move is good for your career, income, or professional advancement. You will feel the loss underneath the sense of satisfaction with the change itself.

As you become more aware of yourself as the person you'd like to become, your priorities will shift. You might start going to church. You might stop going to church. You might change churches. You might make volunteer work a high priority, work-

. . . when you let it

ing with the homeless, hospice patients, or the underprivileged. Or you might make parenting your children or the welfare of a relative your priority. Your life will shift simply because you are experiencing yourself as a different person from the one before. With any of these shifts, you will feel a loss. You might lose interest in watching "the soaps" or NFL football, another type of soap opera. You might lose interest in reading front-page news or watching violent TV shows and movies. You might no longer feel like complaining about what the other drivers are doing, about your job, about people you know, or about anything. From time to time, you could lose some of your vitality, your aliveness. You won't have as much to say about the things that once highly interested you: "soaps," sports, news, politics, TV shows, movies, or many other topics that once seemed important. You will not be as interesting to your old friends, and they won't be as interesting to you. You will have some sense of loss, of being adrift, until your new self takes form. Whatever way this unfolds for you, you will be okay, and you will move towards the realization that you are the person you'd like to become.

THE NEW YOU

Long before you fully realize you are the person you'd like to become, you will feel better in some sense: more at peace with yourself and everyone around you. You will live out of a different set of assumptions. As indicated at the beginning of this chapter, you can expect to know *everything turns out right . . . when you let it*, and recognize the truth of that again and again in your everyday life. You will come to know that the world is a friendly place. And you will live in a spirit of cooperation. You can also expect an increased prosperity consciousness to emerge. This means that as the shift takes place, you will know you have plenty of everything.

You will extend more love to your loved ones, relatives, friends, and co-workers, thereby encouraging them to do the same. On more than one occasion, I have left a particularly challenging business meeting with someone privately complaining to me about one of the participants. My reply was simply, "Just love him." Although this was usually met with disbelief, the message was heard. At future meetings, the participants had less tension and fewer aggravations. Later I heard people who originally scoffed at "Just love him" quote it, partly to be funny and partly because they were beginning to get it.

You will find happiness within yourself to bring to your relationships. You can expect improved health. This might take the form of an end to headaches, release of an allergy, better weight control, excellent response to treatments you receive, or even spontaneous remission. You'll be able to see that you have enough money to do what you need to do.

You will not need to monitor yourself to realize that these things are true. As the new you begins to form, you will feel the difference: lighter, softer, stronger, clearer, and more energetic. You will know your life is changing, and the way you are is more to your liking. You will see more clearly that you are the person you'd like to become.

You need not be afraid of the changes that will take place. Nelson Mandela, President, Republic of South Africa, in his 1994 inaugural speech (attributed to Marianne Williamson) said, "Our deepest fear is not that we are inadequate. Our deepest fear is that we are powerful beyond measure. It is our light, not our darkness, that frightens us. We ask ourselves, who am I to be brilliant, gorgeous, talented and fabulous? Actually who are you not to be? You are a child of God. Your playing small doesn't serve the world. There's nothing enlightened about shrinking so that other people won't feel insecure around you. We were born to manifest the glory of God within us. It's not just in some of us; it's in everyone. And as we let our own light shine, we unconsciously give other people permission to do the same. As we are liberated from our own fear, our presence automatically liberates others."

. . . when you let it

Summary

◇ You are the person you'd like to become.

◇ You need do nothing.

◇ Experience yourself as the person you'd like to become, again and again.

◇ Own your negative feelings, because you can't change what you do not own.

◇ Hold on to the best, let go of the rest.

◇ Realize that what was once threatening you can no longer hurt you.

◇ Let go of negative feelings that come up for you; keep letting go of them until they're gone.

◇ You will experience a sense of loss until your new self emerges.

7

Everything You Do That Comes
from Love, Works

"Love is the answer whatever the question."
—A Course in Miracles

O ne of the things I believe in deeply is *everything you do that comes from love, works.* This is like saying every-thing you do that comes from love turns out right. It cannot be anything but a success. Let's look at some examples.

A FAMILY MOVE

The example that means the most to me is moving to the Tampa Bay area. In 1992, when I started work for the Olin Corporation, Sharon and I were living in Charleston, WV. I was given an office at a chemical plant there, which was my home base for traveling to many Olin locations. The Human Resources manager was a nice guy who took an interest in me, and we often had friendly chats. He and his wife had family in Ohio, and he often told me of his weekend visits to or from the family. I listened to him and to my inner guidance. He was teaching me about love of family without intending to, helping me realize that I missed seeing my daughters, son-in-law, and my grandson, all living in Tampa, FL. Sharon and I would fly down once in a while but we weren't as close as we would like. After two years, it dawned on me that I could do my job just as well, or better, working out of Tampa where the flight schedules were much better than in Charleston, WV. I talked to my boss regarding the possibility of moving and offered to pay for the move. After checking with the appropriate people, he agreed. His approval launched a series of events that made every aspect of the move a pleasure.

In April, on our second house-hunting trip to the Tampa area, we found the perfect house. We had not even put our home in Charleston on the market!

The sellers told us they would be moving into temporary quarters after their house was sold and before the home they were building would be ready. We told them we would like to buy their house at their asking price and asked if they would like to rent it from us until we had our other place sold. We told them we would have to be in by October 31. They agreed, and we closed in June.

Sharon took an adult education course in real estate and put our condo on the market. We assured ourselves that a buyer was looking for just what we had, and that turned out to be the case. We sold our home in Charleston in six weeks at our asking price to people who wanted to move in by August 15. They had sold their home and needed to be out by that date. When we told the people renting our house in Clearwater that we would like to move in by August 15, they said okay. Their house was not going to be ready by October 31, so they would have to find an interim place to live anyway. Besides, a friend of theirs had an empty house they could live in.

The weekend of our move, my daughter Ellen was married in Tampa. When we arrived at our hotel in the wee hours of the morning on Friday, we discovered the hotel where we had reservations had no rooms available. Arrangements had been made for overflow guests to stay at a nearby hotel. We were disappointed. However, when we told the doorman we were hosting the reception on Saturday, the staff found us a room. We were there for the rehearsal dinner on Friday, the wedding and the reception on Saturday, a leisurely Sunday, and a Monday check-out. The moving van arrived Monday afternoon.

I would say our move was beautifully orchestrated, but it wasn't—certainly not by us. The story simply illustrates the principle that everything that comes from love, works. The move to Tampa was out of love for my two daughters, the desire to be closer to them and to help them when we could and help was wanted. The move worked. For the nine years since these events, the move has continued to work. We were on hand for the birth of my granddaughter; we see the grandchildren and their parents regularly, we help them when we can, we see my other daughter from time to time, and have a richer, fuller, more loving life than we could have from Charleston, WV.   For Sharon and me, creating warm, loving relationships with the grandchildren has been wonderful.

A Mother and Son

Another example of these principles comes from a friend and her son. She was a student of *A Course in Miracles*, which emphasizes love ("Teach only love, for that is what you are"). She confided in us that she was having a lot of trouble with her son, a junior in high school, not doing well in his schoolwork. What should she do? I suggested she just love him, and others supported this view. Over the next year and a half, she shared with us the various difficulties she was having because he was not doing well and not qualifying himself for college. She argued frequently with him regarding what he was or was not doing. The question she asked of us was always the same, "What shall I do?" and the answer was always the same, too, "Just love him."

Our friend has four sons; her husband died a few years before we met her. The three older sons were doing well. One was an MD and the head of an anesthesiology department, one was a regional manager for a large national corporation, and the third was a successful car salesman. Our friend wanted her youngest son to go to college and become successful also.

When the young man finished his senior year in high school, he did not meet the requirements for graduation so he went to summer school and received a GED. That fall, he went to college and had to drop out after the first semester. He came home, took a minimum wage job, and started at a local college. That change did not work, so his oldest brother invited him to come live with him and his family in Winchester, VA, attend private school, and prepare himself to do college work. He accepted the invitation, went to the prep school and did well, worked in construction, felt good about himself, went to college, had a "C" average, and left after one year. He had no motivation and did not know what he wanted to do. He felt like he was spinning his wheels, so he left and went home.

Over the seven years I had known my friend, she and her son had developed a better and better relationship. He was working again and feeling uncomfortable because his high school buddies were finishing college and he had not started. He went to North Carolina, worked for a while, and came home to Charleston.

In May 1994, our friend's son called her at work and asked, "Do you know what day this is?"

His mother replied, "No, what do you mean?"

Son: "It's the tenth anniversary of Dad's death. What are you planning to do?"

Mother: "Well, nothing special."

Son: "I'm going out to the cemetery." And he spent much of the day there.

His mother says, "(He) came to my work place and told me about it and how he cried and cried. This was the first time he had talked about his father's death. I think being able to face it and let go helped to put his life in order and move forward."

. . . when you let it

He says "I was employed at a law firm over the summer as a runner. I enjoyed the atmosphere and also enjoyed the intellectual challenges. After being employed for a couple of months, I came to mom and told her I wanted to go into law. She stated that I could become a paralegal, and I told her—No, I was going to law school."

That fall he went back to college, graduated in 1998, started law school that fall, and graduated three years later. In the course of the eleven years between his junior year in high school and his college graduation, our friend let go of her fear of what would happen to her son and just loved him. Together, mother and son illustrated that everything turns out right when you let it. Her love for her son was critical in his transformation from a struggling teenager to an accomplished young man.

A Father and Son

In the summer of 1999, I was having lunch with a business associate and friend. As part of our conversation, he was telling me of struggling in his relationship with his son who seemed to be out of reach. The son was living at home after taking a semester off from college, was not doing anything wrong, but was distant, and my friend did not know how to connect with him. I told him the story of my friend and her son and how he needed to know his mother loved him. For the next few days, my business associate thought about the relationship between the mother and son and gradually realized his son **did** need love from his dad. He softened. A few days later, before my business associate/friend spoke to his son about his change of heart, a miracle happened: his son greeted him with a spontaneous hug! My friend was overjoyed. Their relationship grew stronger, warmer, and deeper.

In the fall, the son went back to college and his dad went to visit him on Columbus Day. They agreed to meet outside of a campus building where the son was getting out of class at noon. My friend arrived in time for the two of them to spot each other from far off and approach each other with broad grins. When they reached each other, dad gave his son a big hug, a loving hug. That afternoon they had a great time together, enjoying what they were doing and each other. My friend told me that the loving relationship he and his son now have grew out of the little seed he planted when he decided to "just love him."

ANOTHER MOTHER AND SON

I have another friend with a struggling teenager. My friend is deeply afraid her talented son will not succeed, and his behavior reinforces those feelings. From time to time, I have counseled her to just love him. She always replies, "I **do** love him," and I know she does. But in all these situations the key word is *just*; *just* love him. The Funk & Wagnall's dictionary helps with understanding this idea. The dictionary defines "*just*, adv. 1 To the exact point, instant, or degree; without lack, excess, or variation; precisely; exactly." In simple words, "just" means not more or less. To just love someone means to extend love without advice, without criticism, without exaggeration, without manipulation, without expecting anything in return, without any concern about the outcome, without any pretense, without anything but love ("the exact point, instant or degree").

UNCONDITIONAL LOVE

To just love someone means giving unconditional love. You might say, "If I were manifesting unconditional love on anything like a regular basis, I probably wouldn't be reading this book." This may be true. The point here is not that you need to achieve perfection. But as we **be**come more loving, act out of our loving nature more, **do** more loving things, we will **have** more loving experiences and relationships. Here the emphasis is on *more*. The experience of unconditional love doesn't come all at once. Each loving thought prepares us for the next one. Each loving thought prepares us for our own loving behavior. Each

. . . when you let it

act of love prepares us for the next loving thought. Each act of love prepares us for desirable outcomes. Every element of the cycle—**be** loving, **do** loving things, **have** the fruits of a loving life —reinforces the other two. After being this way for a while, a few weeks perhaps, you will begin to be aware that "Everything you do that comes from love, works."

What if the world—our friends, relatives, co-workers, or loved ones—doesn't cooperate? What if what we're doing isn't working? What do we do then? We need to look more closely at what is meant by "works." Works doesn't mean having the outcome you thought you wanted. After all, the love we're discussing is unconditional, without any concern with the outcome, which means we can't get the outcome we wanted, because there isn't any; we're operating with no agenda except to extend love. In the previous paragraph, "the fruits of a loving life" are your own feelings of love, compassion, joy, and peace. "Works" means creating those feelings, not as an objective, but as a by-product of extending love. This is an inner experience, **always** available to us as a direct outcome of every loving thing we do.

Out of love for my two daughters and their families, Sharon and I moved to the Tampa Bay area where they all lived. Everything went smoothly for us, as if the events were guided by an unseen hand. I interpret this as evidence that the universe was supporting the move. Without that support, I would question whether to carry out the plan. For example, if we were unable to sell our home in Charleston for an acceptable price, or other events indicated the move was questionable, we would look within ourselves to see whether to move. If one or both of my daughters gave signs they had changed their minds about wanting us to move (parents are not always welcome to live close by), out of love for them we would have sold the house in Florida and stayed in Charleston. And this would have worked! They would have learned we had no hidden agenda, we loved them enough to move to the Tampa Bay area and also, even more, we loved them enough not to move there. My daughters would feel that love, even if they weren't ready to be loved.

everything turns out right . . .

How about us, if we were rejected? The move would work for us too. By being loving; involving them in the process; planning the move out of that love; feeling those feelings of compassion, joy, and peace; having no emotional attachment to the outcome; we get to experience ourselves as loving individuals. We know we have expressed love in a special way. If the move hadn't been right for them at the time we suggested, it would have been okay with us. We could have continued to find ways to extend love to them.

And to keep reminding myself, I often wear a T-shirt imprinted with "Love is the answer, whatever the question," from *A Course in Miracles.*

Over the ten years between the time of her husband's death and her son's transformation, our friend became more and more loving, less and less afraid of what would happen to her son. This is the main story. Her personal transformation came from her love for her son. Her love was what "worked." As she moved toward unconditional love for her son, whether he became a lawyer or even whether he went to college no longer mattered to her. And what mattered to her son was that his mother loved him. Knowing his mother loved him, this bright young man could do what he wanted. And he did.

Conversations with God, Part 1, page 58, "From the highest mountain it has been shouted, in the lowest place its whisper has been heard. *Through the corridors of all human experience has this truth been echoed:* Love is the answer."

. . . when you let it

What if my friend's desire to have a good relationship with his son had been rejected? When he acts out of love as he reaches out to his son, the process works for the father. He becomes a more loving person with all the attendant good feelings. He experiences himself differently, as a loving person. He doesn't need a payoff—a positive response from his son. Those good feelings are the payoff. Once he has broken down his own barriers to being a loving person and expressing love, he can continue to extend love to his son. Whether he receives an overt response doesn't matter much. At some level the son knows his father loves him, and that makes all the difference.

A couple of years ago, my five-year-old granddaughter and Sharon were on the floor playing together, coloring in a book. They had colored together before. At one point the girl looked up and said to Sharon (her step-grandmother), "You really love me, don't you." Sharon replied, "Yes, I love you very much." My reaction was to realize how wonderful this event was. At a young age, my granddaughter knew she was loved. She had learned that at home and now was broadening her awareness of people who loved her. Because Sharon had given her unconditional loving attention for years, she knew she could safely ask. In contrast, I didn't realize my mother loved me until I wrote a eulogy for her after she made her transition at the age of 85. In between these two extremes is my friend's son, at age 20, learning, whether he wants to or not, that he is loved. Happily, he responded positively, but his response was not what made the process work. My friend's love made it work.

What About You?

This principle tells us whatever we do that comes from love will "work." How can we make sure what we do comes from love? By not acting on angry impulses or out of anger of any kind. By not acting out of fear. By giving and not wanting

everything turns out right . . .

anything in return. By giving and not assuming that what we have to give is wanted. By acting compassionately, assuming everyone is doing the best they can. By wanting the other person to get what he or she wants (within reasonable health and safety guidelines) knowing he or she will get what he or she needs. And, ultimately, by listening to our inner guidance, but that's not the easiest place to start. We have another powerful source: our outer experience.

The examples at the beginning of this chapter are from my outer experience; they introduced me to this principle. The story of the mother and son was the first of these. The two of them helped me to open up to the realization that "Everything you do that comes from love, works." The others built upon that foundation. So the place to start is simply to recognize illustrations in your own life that follow this principle. Hold on to them, cherish them, share them with your friends, realize that they describe how the world works. If you find illustrations that don't fit this principle, hold on to them, too. As time goes by and you become more accustomed to this idea, you will find some of the apparent mismatches disappearing. Collect these examples for the rest of your life. We spend most of our waking hours in our outer world, so anchor this principle there. The greater source of strength is in the inner world, but developing it there requires us to give more attention to the illustrations we find in the outer world.

LISTENING TO MY MESSAGES

The computer on which I receive e-mail shares a telephone line with my fax machine; I rarely use the fax, but leave it on so the person wishing to send me a fax can get through instead of getting a busy signal. The faxes just appear unannounced. With the e-mail, however, to get messages, I must do something. I dial up my e-mail access, perhaps two or three times a day. I have e-mail but if I don't turn it on the messages sit out in the memory of some computer.

. . . when you let it

I see an analogy between getting my e-mail messages and getting messages from my inner guidance. As Gregg Levoy, inspirational speaker, has said, I must turn on my receiver. Like everyone else, I have inner guidance available to me, but in order to bring it into consciousness, I have to listen, I have to turn on my receiver. What does that mean? Simply that I have to be alert to the still, small voice within. When I sense promptings, suggestions, or explicit directions appearing in my head, I need to listen up! And when I do what I am being guided to do, I nearly always get good results. The exceptions are the times I follow my guidance and my choice doesn't seem to make any difference. The action I take, or don't take, never turns out badly.

Using Discernment

A common question is, "How can I tell the difference between 'good' inner guidance and my potentially harmful thoughts?" We need discernment. Discernment is different from judgment in that we won't label anything as bad or good. With discernment, we can recognize differences, and in this situation we will know whether the directions we receive are loving. If that is the case, we will want to follow the guidance. In so doing, we are strengthening our ability to see that everything that comes from love, works, by cultivating the love we have within, bringing it into consciousness, and allowing it to work in our outer experience. We want to give love a chance. Listening to our inner guidance in choosing specific things to do virtually assures us love will work. When we find it working in our outer experience, we will place more trust in our inner guidance, and allow ourselves to be more loving. And at times when love is not working the way we'd like in our outer experience, it will surely work in our inner experience; that is, we will be more loving.

INSTANT MESSAGING

The experience of a friend of mine illustrates the idea that we can discover our loving selves virtually in an instant. Sharon and I knew her because she was a member of our *A Course in Miracles* study group. She had a responsible job in a large office and enjoyed her work except for having to work with a woman whom she disliked and who apparently felt the same way towards her. All of their interactions produced friction and irritation. One night, my friend dreamed about this woman, seeing her bathed in white light; my friend was experiencing intense loving feelings. The next morning she saw her co-worker at the office, and without a word *the two of them greeted each other with warmth and friendship; their relationship had been healed and stayed healed until my friend transferred out of their office.* Their relationship was transformed by the instant message my friend received in her dream. In telling this story, my friend's loving experience was deepened and became an important part of who she is. I believe our study of the *Course*, with its emphasis on forgiveness and love, prepared her to have this experience.

Your inner voice and your outer experience will reinforce each other more and more until they create an inner experience of love. To enhance that process, recognize the things you and the people in your life do that come from love. See them working, talk about them, make them a recurring theme in your life. At some point, everything you do will come from love, and everything you do will work.

. . . when you let it

SUMMARY

◈ Everything that comes from love, works.

◈ When loved ones make choices you don't understand, just love them.

◈ Be more loving, Do more loving things, Have more loving relationships.

◈ Love unconditionally.

◈ Turn on your receiver and follow your inner guidance.

◈ Recognize and collect examples of love working in your life and the lives of the people around you.

8

When Life Seems
Overwhelming, Do Less

"In order that people may be happy in their work . . .
they must not do too much of it."
—John Ruskin

The key word here is "seems." Life only *seems* overwhelming; in truth, it isn't. You may feel overwhelmed, but "Life" isn't doing it. If you knew that everything turns out right when you let it, your life wouldn't even seem overwhelming.

LACK OF TALENT OR ABILITY

An adult family friend has told us of having been scared (overwhelmed) at the prospect of going to kindergarten. She was scared because she didn't know how to read and write! Lack of talent or ability is a negative judgment we put on ourselves. We might think we have to make up for this lack by working harder. When we assume or decide something is wrong with us and live out of that assessment, we will feel overwhelmed. Taking on a set of responsibilities or tasks when we feel good about ourselves will not cause us to feel overwhelmed. Taking on the same set when we feel we have a lack of ability will overwhelm us.

Our negative judgment may be incorrect, and we actually have the necessary talent or ability. As with our friend going to kindergarten, we could be totally unrealistic in our judgment and feel overwhelmed as a result. That judgment keeps us from moving forward, keeps us from seeing we are talented. We need to give ourselves a chance.

Of course, we may not have the talent or the ability, and that's all right. A few years ago, the Choir Director asked me to audition for our church choir. The quality of my voice was good, and I had the necessary range. However, I do not read music and, based on past experience, I am a slow learner. I shared that with the Choir Director and was accepted anyway. So I sing in the choir without the talent I would like to have. I enjoy the singing and I'm correcting my mistakes as fast as I can, and looking at what is: in music, I'm a slow learner. From time to time, I give the Choir Director the opportunity to ask me to drop out and he refuses; he wants me to sing in the choir. It's okay for me to do less. By acknowledging my limitations, I am not overwhelmed.

The key to moving past the sense of inadequacy in the talent/ability department is to accept your level of ability, do less, and move forward using the talent and ability you do have. Be willing to learn. You might decide you don't have the talent or ability that's called for, and you're not improving. If that happens, listen for your inner guidance. Every time the issue of your ability comes into your head, ask what is best for you to be doing. Be open to the answer. It won't come to you at once. It may pop into your head when you're waking up or going to sleep; it may be words spoken by someone in your presence; it may be recognition for your talent or ability (an award, raise, or promotion); or you may be given an opportunity in a new field of endeavor. In the meantime, enjoy using the talents you do have.

YOU CAN'T DO MORE

When your life seems overwhelming, you are experiencing tension; it is the number one symptom of being overwhelmed. You might consider relieving your tension by doing more, getting caught up in all you have to do, and thereby creating the opportunity to relax. You might be thinking, "If I could just get all of this stuff done, I could relax." Or, "I'm working more than 50 (or 60) hours a week and not getting everything done. If I could just work an extra 15 or 20 hours for a week or two, I could get caught up and not feel so overwhelmed." Then you would start figuring out how you could work another 15 or 20 hours more a week, etc. Catching up is one approach.

But in fact, the reason we experience life as overwhelming is because we don't know how to find an extra 15 or 20 hours a week. In sports terms, we don't know how to raise the level of our game, and that's all right. If we feel life is overwhelming when working 50 or 60 hours a week, we just can't expect to work another 15 or 20 hours. And beating ourselves up because we're not doing more does not help. We feel overwhelmed by what we're doing and not doing, and we can't do more, so let's do less.

Do Less

What does "do less" mean? Commit to less—commit to less than you have already committed to. Back off from the level of commitment that makes you tense and afraid you're not going to fulfill your commitment, afraid you're not going to do a good job, afraid you're not even going to get started. You could have things you've promised to do and haven't even started yet. We'll discuss those things later, but right now you need a shift.

A shift can occur in the following way. Think of the things you have done over the last year. They could be fun things, fun/risky things, educational things, work things—whatever you were doing. Now imagine that back a year ago you committed to doing only two out of every three things you have already done. Now we realize you did the two things you committed to do, and one extra, which is fifty percent more! Now imagine living that year knowing you were doing the two things you committed to plus the one extra. Feel the feeling. Go into it. Surround yourself with it. Wear it like a rich garment. Fifty per cent more than you committed to! Does that feel overwhelming? No. It feels joyful! So we are describing a shift in perception, in our perception of ourselves, leading to a shift away from being tense to being joyful. The corollary says lower the expectations of yourself, **do less,** and *plan to do even less.* By planning to do even less than you actually will do, you will be an outstanding performer.

In the 1970s, the concept of Management by Objectives (MBO) was introduced into the workplace and is still in use. The idea was to formulate a set of objectives tailored to each person and situation so that everyone had equally challenging assignments. Performance was to be measurable—the dollar value of sales, pounds of goods produced, etc.—so that everyone could easily track progress towards the objectives. Soon bright people figured out they would help themselves by negotiating smaller, easier to reach goals. That is, instead of taking on big, aggressive goals, perhaps making life seem overwhelming, they would opt to *do less.* Because the manager often wanted more sales or more production, the goal-setting process sometimes turned out to be a negotiation between the person whose goals were being set and his or her manager. That was a healthy process. The employees who wanted to stretch themselves and set ambitious goals sometimes found out a little later that life seemed overwhelming. They also needed to *do less.*

As an employee of a large oil company, full of ideas and in love with many of those ideas, I was fortunate in reporting to a boss who frequently responded to my latest idea by asking, "What will you give up doing in order to have time to work on this new idea?" He was helping me avoid being overwhelmed, and we usually succeeded.

But what about the consequences? What if you only committed to doing two out of three things you were "supposed" to do, or "expected" to do? You could be fired, which might be a relief but more likely would make life seem even more overwhelming than before. Planning to be fired does not look like an option, so you commit (in your heart) to doing everything you were asked to do, you look for another job, and you choose not to be overwhelmed. As a result, you might learn: (1) you enjoy your job when you are not overwhelmed; (2) you can meet the challenging goals you and your boss have set; or (3) you can find another job that seems to be less overwhelming.

Another shift in perception that lets you avoid feeling overwhelmed is to see that you don't have to do anything perfectly. You may get perfect results, but you don't have to be the one to create them. You can do your best without stressing yourself by following your inner guidance, knowing that *everything turns out right . . . when you let it.* Keep in mind what a former business associate of mine had to say: "Anything worth doing is worth doing poorly." This adage is much more useful than the one it paraphrases because it frees you to be human and make mistakes. It relieves the pressure of perfectionism.

Can you reasonably expect that when you are not overwhelmed you will enjoy your job and meet its challenging goals? Yes indeed. One of the consequences of feeling overwhelmed is that we resist what is happening. If something is in our way, we resist instead of sliding around the obstacle. If we're asked to do one more thing, we don't even want to think about it. If circumstances change—a new goal, a new path—we experience a lot of frustration and resistance towards "them." All that resistance shows up in our body language and in our thought processes. Whatever we do takes more energy simply because we have to overcome that resistance. It slows us down and even wears us out; our resistance can make life seem overwhelming. So, when we are functioning without being overwhelmed—comfortable, strong, confident—we will achieve better results and maybe meet challenging goals.

BEING OVERWHELMED IS A CHOICE

Changing our perception of what we're doing, as suggested above, is a symptomatic treatment. Before looking into the

everything turns out right . . .

basic, down-deep causes of feeling overwhelmed, let us acknowledge that feeling overwhelmed is a choice coming from inside us, not from "out there." "Overwhelming" starts with a judgment on our part, which is why the corollary says **seems** to be overwhelming. When we follow the teachings of J. Krishnamurti, we simply, "Look at what is." We look at what is going on in our lives without judgment, without interpretation, without explanation, without analysis, without naming it, and without blaming anyone, especially ourselves. Whenever I am stressed or upset, with little or no effort and without blaming myself, I can always find the cause within myself. You can, too.

How can you do that? Be open and honest with yourself. Be open to the possibility that *you* are the true source of your feelings of being overwhelmed. Be honest regarding your responsibility for those feelings. Realize you may have created an environment for yourself in which feelings of being overwhelmed can grow, blossom, and even run rampant.

The remainder of this chapter discusses seven possible causes for feeling overwhelmed and how to avoid that feeling. Notice whether any of them apply to you; this is an important step towards moving past whatever you're doing to feel overwhelmed. If one or more of the payoffs do apply, you can use future feelings of being overwhelmed as signposts pointing towards the self-perception, the behaviors, and the priorities creating the environment for you to feel that way.

When your life seems overwhelming, instead of feeling helpless, you can recall that your fear of not having enough (time, money, appreciation, recognition) is what you bring to the experience. You can choose to let go of the fear. As you do this, your feelings of being overwhelmed will diminish and, if you continue this practice, disappear.

LACK OF MONEY, DENIAL

If you accept the fact that you lack the money you need to do the things you want to do, you can just do your job and enjoy

. . . when you let it

your paycheck. You can choose to set aside your wants, including how you want to provide for your family. Or you can choose to pursue supplemental income. You can follow your inner guidance towards prosperity.

If you don't accept the fact that you lack the money you need to do the things you want to do, if you deny it, you must work feverishly to cover it up. If you are in denial about your lack of money, you won't even know you're working feverishly to cover it up. You'll just feel overwhelmed. And the source of that stress is neither lack of money nor the many things we do to overcome our sense of lack of money; it's the perception that something is wrong, that we're not doing enough. (See *Painting the House* in Chapter 3.)

FEELING OVERWHELMED AS A CONTROLLING BEHAVIOR

The sense of being overwhelmed is not the cause of controlling behavior—it is simply a choice made by people who have a need to be in control. This is true even for people who say, "My life is completely out of control!"

How is it possible that people who have a need to be in control would choose to be overwhelmed? Those who are *very busy* can choose not to do anything they're asked to do simply because they are so busy. On the other hand, they can still choose to take on any additional tasks or activities they want. Busy people are very much in control of what they do. Anyone who sees life as overwhelming can benefit from looking within to search for a control issue behind that perception. Notice that for people who have a need to be in control, the *idea* of being overwhelmed is appealing because it acts like a filter to reject unpleasant or unwanted tasks.

But the *reality* of being overwhelmed is difficult. When life seems overwhelming to you, consider whether giving up control and going with the flow has any appeal for you. If you go with the flow, you will naturally do less.

everything turns out right . . .

I have known several people who have exhibited this behavior. They were managers, senior technical people, and organizational leaders. It was difficult for them to take on new tasks because they were too busy (overwhelmed), and yet they could always do one more thing that interested them.

A NEED FOR ALIVENESS

For some people, a high level of activity is the norm. One of these is a little person—my seven-year-old granddaughter—whose natural pace is double-time. Any time she moves from one place to another, she trots or runs. This is true even when she's at home just going from one room to another. In her dance class number in a recent recital, she danced with great verve. When the number was over, the dozen or so children walked off the stage with their music playing in the background. All except my granddaughter, who went off with them, still dancing as energetically and joyously as ever, with feet doing the steps, head bobbing, and arms pumping. She did not feel overwhelmed; she did not need to do less; she was at the top of her world and very much alive. So a high level of activity does not have to lead to a feeling of being overwhelmed.

Some people, however, must be busy in order to feel fully alive. They must be doing something: working, playing with their children, fund-raising for their church, working more, playing or coaching some sport, taking family trips, going to school, working still more, leading civic organizations, entertaining, web-surfing, channel-surfing, and more. Each of these can be a healthy activity. The nature of these activities does not make life seem overwhelming; it is the total time and energy we give to them. In my forties, I went to the hospital with a health challenge. I needed to cut back on my activities. I was doing the list above (except for the last two surfing items) with heavy emphasis on work and leading civic organizations. I was surprised to learn how much I was doing. I wasn't aware of feeling overwhelmed, but my body was and expressed this as acute asth-

. . . when you let it

ma. Until then, I had lived as if I needed all that activity in order to feel fully alive. At that point, I accepted my body's opinion and gave up all my non-essential activities.

I didn't realize at the time that I could feel fully alive in a contemplative state, which leads to heightened awareness. And if I could feel fully alive in a contemplative state, I certainly could with any level of activity.

You can, too. Your aliveness depends only on how you experience what you are doing. Do you see or hear the subtleties in people's expressions revealing whether they are happy, sad, well, or ill? Do you respond to what you see and hear? Are you compassionate? Loving? Supportive? Do you know what you're doing? What are you building?

A man came upon three bricklayers who all seemed to be doing the same thing. He asked the first what he was doing and the reply came,

"Laying brick."

The passerby walked a few more steps and asked the second worker what he was doing.

"Building a wall," he said.

The walker went on a few more steps and asked the third man what he was doing. He looked up with a smile and said,

"Building a cathedral."

The truth is, we're all building cathedrals. We're helping to create magnificent adults from little children. We're building stronger and more beautiful relationships, teams, organizations, companies, churches, and communities. When we know we're building these cathedrals, we will feel fully alive. We will not need to seek out so many tasks and responsibilities that we feel overwhelmed. But what if these seek us out?

everything turns out right . . .

THE DESIRE TO BE A SUPERSTAR OR SUPERMOM

For some people, the path to feeling overwhelmed is the desire to be a superstar or supermom, to look good. These people welcome the invitation or request to do one more thing. Just that much—the opportunity to do more—causes their adrenaline to flow. Lead the troop, coach the team, take the trip, make the costumes, relocate for three months, lead the fund drive, stay late, host the family dinner—all have great appeal to the superstar or supermom. What can you do? "Just say no." That's what we tell our children so they will avoid addictions. When we recognize our need for achievement is a fix to keep us feeling fully alive, we will know we must "Just say no" the next time we're asked.

A friend of mine had an experience illustrating the down side of saying no. He said no by retiring in his fifties after years as a highly successful business executive. Throughout his career, he'd been a superstar, fully alive and aware of his aliveness. A member of top management, he'd planned, led, directed, negotiated, and inspired with great personal and professional competence as well as corporate success. Within a year after retirement, he was sitting in his backyard enjoying the magnificent view and saying to himself, "My life is over." He was experiencing the pain of withdrawal from the powerful drug he had been on for a long time: achievement. Since then, he has moved past those feelings. Both his achievements and his decision to say no are wonderful. Furthermore, they teach us that, if we have been on a high as a superstar or supermom, we can expect withdrawal pains. (The "empty nest" syndrome is a collection of these feelings.) When we do choose to say no because life seems overwhelming, we can expect the withdrawal process to be a little more severe because we still have the alternative of going back and being overwhelmed again. We always have that choice.

. . . when you let it

I'm Not Good Enough

For many people, the path to feeling overwhelmed is low self-esteem. Those people dread the invitation, request, or directive to do one more thing. They dread it because they think they're supposed to say "yes." They feel the need to prove that they can do what is being asked of them, and they're afraid they can't, especially because they are already overwhelmed. They resent the demands and requests made of them.

If you ever find yourself in this situation, you can help yourself enormously by seeing that no one is forcing you to do anything. Realize that you are choosing to accept each "opportunity" instead of working out a better response to directives, demands, and requests. In many cases, accepting whatever opportunity comes along is the best course to take, but not out of a sense of "I have to." And recognize that **you are good enough**, even better than that, otherwise you wouldn't be the person selected to do this next thing.

In my first engineering job, I worked as a technical salesman in an office. After a while, having fallen behind in my paperwork, I stayed late after dinner—until 2:00 a.m. I cleaned up the backlog and left a pile of completed work in my outbox. The next morning, the office secretary picked up my work and asked me what I had done. When I told her, she went to the president's office, arms full, to tell him excitedly what I had accomplished. His response was that if I couldn't get my work done during regular hours, I *ought* to be working till 2:00 a.m. This had the potential for instilling in me the sense that I was not good enough. At that point in my life, without understanding much about the way life works, I realized that his response was about him and not me. So I let go, avoiding the feeling that I was not good enough.

In contrast, a woman I know worked for a government social service agency for eight years, becoming gradually more and more burdened by unfinished paperwork and concerns about her clients. She didn't want to give up time in the field with her clients to complete her paperwork, yet was not allowed to return to her office to do it after hours or take it home on weekends. She began to have trouble sleeping, and her job gradually took over her life. She was not willing to quit this draining job because she felt her clients needed her. One day, a client asked her to do something that would require breaking an agency rule. Reluctantly, she agreed to do it to temporarily help out the client. Her action was discovered and she was fired. That was the only way she could get herself out of the situation that was overwhelming her.

This woman never felt she was doing enough for her clients. If she had enjoyed a better perception of herself and what she was accomplishing, she might have had a more balanced view of her job, of what she could and could not do for her clients, of what was required of her by the agency. She might have been able to release being overwhelmed, keep up with the paperwork, and derive more pleasure out of the time she did spend with her clients.

DOING FOR OUR CHILDREN

This can often lead to feelings of being overwhelmed. The necessity or choice to have two incomes to support the family, single parenthood, single parenthood and working two jobs, increasingly upscale lifestyles for children, and other factors contribute to the stress of doing for our children. Parents today feel the need, sometimes the intense need, to have more time and more money for their children. Often those two conflict. To have more money, parents might need to spend more time at work, taking all the available overtime, or find a second job, which means less time with the children. Parents often feel overwhelmed trying to balance having more time and more money for their children.

Three guiding principles help with this apparent dilemma:

1. A principle propounded by Sophia Fahs more than 60 years ago is still valid today: "The method is the meaning." It was

. . . when you let it

created to be the context for teaching Sunday school lessons in Unitarian churches. How the children are taught matters more than what lesson is taught. The principle applies to all interactions between adults and children.

2. As we learn from *A Course in Miracles*, all of us are teaching all the time. We are told we can choose whether we will teach love or fear and advised to "Teach only love, for that is what you are." So the second principle for relating to our children, introduced in the previous chapter, is: "just love them." How we relate to our children is the meaning they get. What we do for our children is not so important; how we do it and who we are matter the most.

3. The third principle is to notice more how we are being with our children and less what we are *do*ing for them. If we are overwhelmed and stressed, we are extending less love than we wish and the children need. Anytime you experience stress with your children, stop what you're *do*ing (do less) and be more tender, loving, and compassionate. Just love them; don't try to fix them, not right now. If you must physically restrain them to do what needs to be done or to keep them from harming themselves or others, do so with minimum force while whispering, "I love you," again and again. Be in touch with the love you have for them, so that "I love you" comes from your heart, not your head.

EXERCISE: LETTING GO

Think of a period of time when you felt overwhelmed. It might be a week, a month, or a year. Get in touch with the negative feelings you had then, perhaps self-doubt, fear of failure, or anxiety.

Now let those feelings go and focus on what you accomplished during that period of time. Realize that this is all you *had* to do. Appreciate the value of what you did. Enjoy those accomplishments.

Now let those feelings go and focus on what you did not accomplish that you wanted to during that period of time. Make it okay. Realize that you didn't have to do any of those things. Notice the difference in your life when you know you don't have to do things you are not going to do. That perspective is always available to you. It's okay to do less.

Summary

◈ When life seems overwhelming, you can't do more. Do less.

◈ Commit to doing even less.

◈ "Overwhelming" is a perception.

◈ Being overwhelmed is a choice.

◈ When life seems overwhelming, let those feelings of tension— a headache or backache perhaps—guide you to the source of discomfort.

◈ We are all building cathedrals.

9

If You Reach
the End of Your Rope,
Let Go and Fly

*"Insanity is continuing to do the same thing
and expecting a different result."*
—Mike Wickett

This principle underscores the . . . *let it* of the basic principle: *Everything turns out right . . . when you let it.* Let's start out looking at letting go of things we know we're holding on to: an unsatisfactory relationship, job, or career, or a negative self-image. Then we'll look at letting go of things we might not know we're holding on to. Here *fly* means to move on, unencumbered by the things that are not working. Flying brings with it the sense of joy and exhilaration we experience in a small airplane or a flying dream.

I Flew

After being engaged in research and development at a large oil company for ten years, I started writing a technical book for the company. I worked on it for five years. Although I was given the opportunity to write the book and was highly regarded, my professional advancement was not going well. So when I was four months from completing it, I decided to leave the company when I finished my book if no major development occurred in my career. Shortly thereafter, I received a gift from the Universe: the management offered to relocate me to Los Angeles for a job I had already said I didn't want. I objected to the job, not the location. When I asked for the job I *did* want (at that same location), I was turned down.

Many subsequent discussions with the management convinced me they were not going to advance my career the way I wanted them to. That was the gift. I was able to resign, free of doubt, after I finished the book. I had been in the same job for nine years, and I had reached the end of my rope. I let go to form my own consulting business, and this completely changed my life. I grew personally and spiritually in ways I had never imagined. I now believe a part of me knew the nature of the journey I was undertaking; the day I resigned, I was trembling even though I was doing the right thing.

My Picture

A cliff has about ten feet of sturdy rope dangling over the edge, hanging down. In the vertical portion of the cliff, a tree grows out of a crack in the rock, perpetually bent by the force of the wind. A thirty-something woman is at the end of the rope dressed in early 20th century garb with a long loose skirt and a hat with a brim. She's looking down at the valley floor, some 1000 feet below, reminding me of the old silent movie series, *The Perils of Pauline.* Each week, Pauline would be caught in some desperate, life-threatening situation, and the following week she would be saved or would extricate herself from her predicament, giving us the term "cliff-hanger." The woman in my picture doesn't seem to have any terror in her gaze, she's just looking down. This could be a painting entitled, "At the End of Her Rope."

The idea of this picture representing the theme of this chapter seems incongruous because this woman clearly cannot actually fly, and if she lets go she'll fall and be hurt. On taking a closer look, we see that the woman is not being threatened and she is holding on to the rope with a lot of strength. Apparently she could climb up the rope and reach the top of the cliff, out of danger, but she shows no sign of doing so.

Whether you are male or female, imagine yourself at the end of that rope, dangling over the cliff. Looking down, you see the abyss, with the valley floor far below. Looking up, you only see ten feet of rope disappearing over the lip of the overhang. Looking to the right, you see the tree clinging to the side of the cliff face. Looking to the left, you see only naked rock. You have reached the end of your rope; how do you feel? Are you scared? Desperate? Angry? Are you praying, "Dear God, if You get me out of this, I promise I will . . ." Or, "Dear God, what shall I do?"

In tough situations, I have often been helped after I have LET GO and admitted to myself and to the Universe that I couldn't do for myself. I have told Holy Spirit, "I can't do this myself, I need help." Then I'd let go, and the answers would come.

In terms of cliff-hanging, the answers might be one of the following:

◊ She can swing on the rope from side to side and help herself by kicking the cliff wall, until she swings over to the tree and climbs to safety. (She's seeing something she had previously overlooked.)

◊ She can use her hands and feet to climb the rope to the edge of the cliff and clamber to safety. (The direct approach can work.)

◊ She can call out as loudly as she can to attract helping hands. (She's not in this alone, and someone will help her.)

How will you receive suggestions like these? By knowing you don't know the answer. By expecting an answer. By being still. By listening to your silent inner voice. By being open to whatever comes. By not being afraid of what the answer might be. By trusting that an answer will come and will work for you and for everyone else. And, when you are no longer at the end of your rope, regardless of how you got out of the situation, you will feel so free and wonderful that you will fly.

TRUSTING YOUR GUIDANCE

How can you develop trust in the answers and in the guidance you receive? By practicing. By turning over lots of choices and decisions to your inner guidance and choosing the answers you receive. By not making choices out of fear of the consequences. By being predisposed to making decisions out of love so when the answers you receive are loving ones, you will easily choose them. As you choose to act on the answers you receive, you and your inner guidance will develop rapport. Out of those decisions will come trust in the answers and in the guidance you receive. Then, if you should ever reach the end of your rope, you will confidently look to your inner guidance for the answer that will work for you and for everyone else. Inner guidance is like a muscle. The more you use it, the more often and more powerfully it will work for you.

CELEBRATE!

Let's suppose you find yourself at the end of the rope and you ask for help. You receive guidance, you follow it, and suddenly you're up and over the edge of the cliff. How do you feel? Like dancing, jumping and shouting for joy? You might be filled with gratitude. Tears of joy might come to your eyes. You might feel like you are flying! If this happens, holding back those good feelings or worrying about whether this cliffhanging experience could repeat itself will diminish your personal growth, especially your ability to receive and accept guidance. Instead, celebrate! Dance! Jump for joy! Acknowledge and give thanks to the Universe for your deliverance! Share the news of your good fortune with friends, relatives, co-workers, and everyone you meet! Own the entire experience, from reaching the end of your rope to flying.

. . . when you let it

An Illustration

While writing this chapter, I had a wonderful experience illustrating the principle of listening to inner guidance. In preparation for writing this chapter, I had made several notes on specific personal examples, and that was all. When I was ready to write, I read those notes and realized I didn't know what I was going to write. Only the image of the woman at the end of her rope came to mind; I remembered seeing that image before. I had no idea how it was going to fit with this theme because it seemed a little bizarre. But I knew the picture came for me so I mentally shrugged, typed, and continued typing for hours. I knew what to write! A couple of times I was overcome by emotion, not from what I was writing but from the beauty of the process. I was being given an illustration as I wrote.

Taking Control

Contrary to my first thought, when I'm at the end of my rope, I've lost control. When I let go and fly, I've taken back control. Over whom? Over what? Myself, and I am now in a position to follow my inner guidance. To say, "I have reached the end of my rope," usually means doing things I don't want to do. I'm letting someone else run my life, and I am *playing the victim.* This is not fun play or child's play. Although I have chosen the victim role for myself, I don't like the way I feel. I may mightily resist being in that role but, until I let go, I won't get my life back.

You can expect you'll never reach the end of your rope while you're following your inner guidance and acting out of love for yourself and everyone you encounter every day. So, let no one take charge of your life except yourself; act out of love for yourself and everyone you encounter every day.

THE END OF YOUR ROPE: RELATIONSHIPS, JOBS AND CAREER

How do we reach the end of our rope in relationships, jobs, or career? They start out full of promise, we start out full of expectations, and then one, five, ten, twenty years later, something has changed. We may think everything has changed. What was once a great source of joy is now a great struggle. Regardless of what we do or don't do, our sense of well-being continues to spiral downward. Down and down until we reach the end of our rope. How can we let go? This relationship, job, career has been our life! A substantial part of life is composed of relationships. How can we let go of ours?

Who would you be if you weren't your spouse's wife or husband, someone's significant other, someone's best friend, a loyal employee where you've worked all these years, or a lawyer, a teacher, an engineer, an executive, a sales representative? You may not know. Despite this uncertainty, if you reach the end of your rope, you must let go. If you don't, you can't move forward.

How will you know you're at the end of your rope? If you don't know, you're not there. You don't have to figure it out. You know when you're at the end of your rope. Listen to your inner guidance for ways to improve the relationship, the job, or the career; be open to what you receive; be willing to change your mind about the situation, allowing it to improve; ignore your desire to make the other person or the organization wrong; let go of feelings of hostility and resentments; erase any line you have drawn in the sand; and, most important of all, act on the guidance you receive to improve the situation. If you do all this for weeks or months and the situation does not improve substantially, or if you usually feel like a victim, you will know you're at the end of your rope.

With a single exception, I have quit every one of my jobs, seven resignations in all. This is despite being raised during the Depression when my family's plan for me was to go to college, become an engineer, go to work for a good company, and retire

. . . when you let it

from that same company at age 65. I broke out of that mold on graduation day, leaving college with an engineering degree and no job. The first post-World War II recession had started and jobs were scarce. In a few months, I was given a job, then a few years later another, and another. Each of the jobs was better than the previous one, and I was not without a job for even a single day; the process enabled me to grow in ways I could not have done otherwise. Sometimes I reached the end of my rope, while at other times I simply looked around to discover what else was available and was offered an opportunity I couldn't refuse. In each case, I was open to the possibilities.

This principle is illustrated by the realtor who found the poster she wanted, as described in Chapter 2. I contacted her to obtain permission to include her story. She sent me this e-mail: "The realtor was at the end of her rope and, seeing Charlie's Law™ [for the first time] she let go! It was then, after a year of being a realtor, that she got her first listing . . . a million dollar one at that! When at the end of your rope, I can promise letting go is the only answer."

HOW DO WE LET GO?

First, by choosing to let go. When your inner guidance says, "It's time for you to let go," and you say, "Yes," the process has begun. Then you must do the things letting go requires: look for a place to live after the relationship is over, tell the other person the relationship is over, look for another job, or choose another career. Then at some point, the physical separation will be complete and the real letting go can begin. Each time you think about the other person, job, or career, you can expect emotions to come up. Even the people who have left the relationship or quit the job are likely to have the emotions associated with any loss: anger ("Why couldn't it have been different, more the way I wanted it to be?"), grief, disappointment, guilt, remorse, and/or depression. And when you think about who or what you've let go of, you might have physical sensations: butterflies

everything turns out right . . .

in the stomach or tightness in the jaw, neck, chest, or abdomen. All of this in reaction to *you* letting go!

To let go, own the emotions. Remind yourself you have chosen to let go for your own good. In thinking about the other person or situation, assume everyone, including you and the other person, is doing the best he or she can. Recognize the truth of that. The other, like the rest of us, could be more loving. Forgive him. Bless her. Extend love to him or her. As you leave the relationship or job, be compassionate. The other person is hurting, not because you have let go, but because of what is going on inside of him or her. Your letting go is the right thing to do. Being loving towards the people or organization you're letting go of will help you let go. Letting go will help you be more loving. Everything is okay. "But," you might say, "I still love that woman," (or the man, or the job). That's okay too; just remember: it's not the right one for you; continue to let go.

Can you ever go back? Yes, after all the people involved have let go of all the hurts, and they have been healed.

Own your physical reactions too. Relax your jaw, neck, chest, and abdomen, wherever you feel tightness. Notice that as days, weeks, and months go by, these become less intense. Relax them every time you feel tension in them. You will find it easier to forgive the others and bless them. The sensations will become still less intense and finally disappear. Then you will know you have let go.

WHAT ELSE ARE YOU HOLDING ON TO?

Lost loves (someone who has let go of you), old hurts, cherished opinions, need to control, circumstances, negative thoughts and judgments, preferences, habitual behaviors, sexual stereotypes, and prejudices. We need to let go of them for the same reasons we might need to let go of a relationship—to reduce stress, and for our emotional, mental, spiritual, and physical well being.

. . . when you let it

Lost Loves and Old Hurts

Sometimes we hold on to lost loves or old hurts. Your response may be, "I don't!" Do you ever think about your lost love or your old hurt? If you do, do you extend forgiveness to your lost love or to the ones who created the old hurt? Do you wish them well? Have you acknowledged your role in the relationship? Have you forgiven yourself for your role? If your answers to these questions are "Yes!" you are not holding on.

When you think about your loss or hurt, do you feel some anger, resentment, frustration, or other negative emotions? In the last weeks, have you gone over in your mind what your lost love did to you or what the old hurt was about? If so, did you have a sense of being a victim, being treated unfairly or unjustly? Do you now, as you read this? Do you ask "Why?" with frustration or anguish? If one or more negative emotions are gripping you, you have not let go. They can't grip you unless you hold on. If you let go and fly, they can't touch you.

Ask yourself, "Why haven't I let go? What's the payoff for me hanging onto the painful relationship?" Some people are holding on to situations and having sporadic angry outbursts providing energy for their aliveness. The energy is the payoff for them; the pain is part of who they think they are. Others are heavily invested in being "right." They hold on to their lost loves and old hurts in order to make them wrong.

Still others have personalities that include not feeling good about themselves. They hold on to their rope because their suffering fits their poor self-image. They hold on to their poor self-image because it justifies not being wonderful, loving, beautiful, energetic people—a scary circumstance.

Opinions

A quote from the practice of quality management: "An opinion without data (facts) is just another opinion." An opinion is something we make up to explain some piece of the universe to ourselves and perhaps to others. By its very nature, it lacks certainty; that is, any opinion could be wrong. Our well being requires we not hold on to our opinions too tightly or invest in them too heavily.

Offering our opinions or sharing them is healthy for our audience and ourselves but, once that is done, we must let them go and let the truth decide what's right. Let them go, listen to others' opinions, and learn. Make it okay that someone else disagrees with us or has just the opposite point of view. It helps to *know* that differences in opinions are okay. Know that some opinions are rooted in the egos of the people who hold them, including you and me. So, in order to let go of our opinions, we may have to give up part of ourselves. This can be painful and hard.

NEED TO CONTROL

Our need to control is rooted in our fear that something not so good, or even bad, will occur if we don't control what is happening. A need to control denies *everything turns out right . . . when you let it.* It denies the role of the Universe in shaping our lives. It denies the inner voice guiding us through our decisions and actions.

To let go of the need to control, you must trust the guidance you receive. Practicing on everyday issues and watching the outcomes allow you to see that those outcomes are okay. Then it will become easier for you to relinquish control over your life and the people around you.

CIRCUMSTANCES AND HISTORY

Many circumstances shape our lives. Birth defects, congenital diseases, physically debilitating diseases, mental diseases, how we were brought up, trauma, crippling accidents, and other less stressful circumstances all affect our view of life. Should we let go of them? Can we let go of them? The answer to both questions seems to be "Yes."

. . . when you let it

I experienced only mildly difficult circumstances. The one I didn't experience is the most valuable to me. I grew up in New York City during the Depression. My father was unemployed a lot, and we had little money. When I was five years old, my parents, my older sister, and I moved to a one-bedroom apartment. When the three of them were ready to go to bed, I was carried into the living room to sleep on the couch. Some of our meals were quite skimpy. I didn't experience this as mildly difficult because I didn't know we were poor. I just thought we were doing what everyone was doing. This lasted for six years, and I never did know we were poor. I was too young to appreciate it, but my parents gave me a lesson in perception. Since no one told me we were poor, I didn't experience poverty, as such, just a cramped apartment and some skimpy meals. And, in the midst of our limited abundance, my parents talked of me becoming an engineer.

Others have had far more difficult and painful circumstances than I. However, we all can help ourselves by letting go of the *circumstances* of our situation and any *comparisons* with how others are doing or what society thinks of what we're doing. When we let go of the origins of circumstances—what caused them and who's to blame—and focus on who we are, we will alleviate the suffering and open a window to personal development. Where appropriate, we will mitigate the pain and make use of every resource and capability, and never look back. We have some shining examples of tremendous inner strength enabling people to transcend their circumstances. In spite of being deaf and blind, Helen Keller learned to speak and read, and to become a strong advocate for the blind. Franklin D. Roosevelt became president of the United States after he was unable to walk due to paralysis brought on by polio. Christopher Reeve became a powerful spokesman for quadriplegics after severing his spinal cord. Lance Armstrong won the grueling Tour de France bike race five times in a row after being given six months to live with testicular cancer. Each one let go and learned to fly.

everything turns out right . . .

PREFERENCES

Hey! What's wrong with preferences? Why would you want to let go of your preferences? Because if you own them as if they were your core values, they will be in the way of being who you are. You certainly are not your preferences. You are a loving, caring person. Think of planning a meal at home. If your preference is to have beans for dinner and a family member prefers corn, why would you not want them to have corn? If you were a guest at someone's home and were served corn, you'd probably eat it, perhaps taking a small portion if you don't like corn. Why not at home? What if the beans you want are on hand and serving corn would require a trip to the store? Could you let go of your idea that going to the store would take too much time and energy and say, "We don't have any corn. Would you like me to go to the store and get some?" Or "Would you like to go to the store and get some?" or "What would you like instead of corn?" or "Would it be okay to have beans tonight and corn tomorrow night?"

Each of these loving gestures or offers is liberating. When extended throughout your life to all of your shared activities—meals, church events, work assignments, movies, clubs, TV programs, restaurants, friends—living this way is like flying. You don't have to suppress your preferences, just be ready to let go of your grip on them.

Do you feel peaceful, knowing you don't have to compete to have your preferences honored? Do you feel loving knowing you are continually giving? Or are you afraid that other people will take advantage of you? If you don't feel peaceful and loving, maybe a part of you wants to be validated by others. This is a risky business because you are placing your sense of well-being in the hands of someone else. "If you really loved me, you would agree to have beans tonight" sounds a little strange, but that's where we are when we hold on too tightly to our preferences.

Living at home with my parents, I learned to wait for things to be offered to me. This was a way of life. As an adult, I became more competitive at work and home, and in sports. I became more attached to my preferences, struggling to get what I wanted. Now I understand the principle of Chapter 2 (if I need something, it will come to me). I don't need to have preferences, just notice what comes to me. It's wonderful.

HABITUAL BEHAVIORS

Habitual behaviors are the opposite of acting in accordance with our inner guidance. Habits are convenient because they don't require any thought, sometimes leading to thoughtless acts. They impede our personal growth because they don't allow us to be creative in our response to what's going on in our lives. And, "If we always do what we've always done, we'll always get what we always got."

The creativity will come in the way we experience who we are. If we hold on to the rope called "Our Behaviors," we will have difficulty allowing any shift to take place. If on the inside we become more loving, and outside we are holding on to hurtful/unloving behaviors, we will be resisting the changes necessary to integrate who we are with how we behave. That is, we can't live out of new-found love, compassion, and inner peace if we are automatically responding to events the way we always have. As described in Chapter 6, I had to give up negative humor—which was hard to do because I thought I was very funny—in order to experience myself as a more loving person. And the development unfolded in that order: I let go of the negative humor and then flew.

People seem to exhibit three kinds of behaviors, based on habits, analysis, and inner guidance. You will live more and more joyfully as you move from behaviors coming from habits to those resulting from analysis of each situation, and finally to those that are responses to inner guidance. Will you reach the point where you have new habitual behaviors based upon love, compassion, and inner peace? Yes, and when you rely on your inner guidance, those "habitual behaviors" will evolve into higher expressions of you.

everything turns out right . . .

What About Elderly Parents, Children, and Others for Whom You Are Responsible?

What if you are a caregiver and reach the end of your rope? Can you let go and fly? Not in the sense of abandoning your responsibilities as caregiver. But you can in another sense. Choose not to be burdened by the responsibilities. Let go of judgments of the situation. Let go of feelings of being victimized. Get in touch with the love you have for the ones you care for. Know that you are a blessing to them, even if they don't. Recognize yourself as an inspiration to those around you who are noticing what you are doing.

Over the years, Sharon and her mother had a relationship that became draining of Sharon's energy. Finally, Sharon let go and flew. A year later, her mother fell and shattered her hip. Sharon's sister Kathy commuted from another state to act as caregiver for their mother while she was recovering in a nursing home. Sharon helped. Before the physical therapy for the hip was complete, their mother was diagnosed with untreatable lung cancer. Kathy continued to be the principal caregiver, and Sharon was her relief, spending a week or two at a time 800 miles from home.

Sharon's other sister, Janet, who also lived far away, had been long estranged from their mother. Realizing her mother's health was failing, she let go of the past, accepted her mother, and came to visit and provide respite for Kathy.

Sharon and Kathy's care lasted several months, and created a supportive environment for their mother's transition. Towards the end, the social worker visiting their mother said he had never witnessed such devoted care as the daughters had provided. Where did that care come from? From the love flowing among sisters and between mother and daughters, more love than they had ever experienced. Having let go and flown, Sharon was free to create a loving relationship with her mother. As a result, she and her sisters were an inspiration and a blessing to those around them. But Sharon had to let go first.

. . . when you let it

How Can I Avoid
Reaching the End of My Rope?

We want to live in peace and with love. We don't want to reach the point where we're dangling at the end of a rope looking down at a thousand-foot sheer drop. How can we avoid reaching the end of the rope?

The best things we can do for ourselves are to be alert (mindful) and open to change. We reach the end of the rope inch by inch, not all of a sudden and, at some level, we know what is going on. The expression "painting myself into a corner" gives us a useful image. We will not trap ourselves like that if we are paying attention to what we're doing. We must be aware of what is going on, what we're doing, before the last doorway and window are painted. In everyday life, "paying attention" certainly includes listening to our inner voice and following the guidance we are given. Not being afraid to follow our guidance is a critical factor in not reaching the end of our ropes. The following personal story illustrates the point.

I had a job in Charleston, WV, and had a feeling something wasn't right although, on the surface, everything seemed to be going just fine. Listening to the small voice within, I decided to leave my job as operations manager of a start-up organization. In my head I thought I was doing a good job, but I did not have that experience in my real life. I did not have that feeling. I tried to change what I thought needed to be changed, but nothing happened. I decided to leave the job, to let go and fly. I moved to a new job where I could live more joyously.

At that point I discovered that nobody cared. I was leaving and nobody cared! My boss accepted my resignation over the phone, and he did not have time to meet with me before I left, or even have lunch with me. The top man in the organization told me over the phone after he knew I was leaving, "Let's have lunch sometime," and four years later we had that lunch. I was able to let go, stop agonizing over whether the organization was succeeding or I was succeeding, and fly. This move opened up

everything turns out right . . .

travel and contacts with hundreds of people with whom I shared ideas and from whom I learned a lot. I let go and flew.

A business associate/friend of mine was the manager of a medium-sized manufacturing facility. He was frequently contacted by executive search people wanting to interest him in employment opportunities with their clients. He always declined. That is, until one day when he decided to follow up on one of the inquiries. The job being discussed was one for which he was well qualified, and it sounded interesting to him. By the time he received a job offer, he was becoming increasingly aware that the scope of his current job was being dramatically reduced and he was being asked to do more with less. The experience was frustrating and unrewarding. So he accepted the offer. By being open to his intuition (his inner guidance), he avoided reaching the end of his rope.

. . . when you let it

Summary

◊ If you reach the end of your rope, let go and fly.

◊ Look at what you know you're holding on to: relationships, job, self-image, and other facets of your life.

◊ It is safe to assume that everyone's doing the best they can . . . and that includes you.

◊ Look at what you might not know you're holding on to.

◊ Look at the payoff for holding on.

◊ When you're at the end of your rope, you've lost control of your life; take it back.

◊ Develop trust in your inner guidance.

◊ Be alert and open to change.

◊ Notice that the physical sensations you have associated with holding on will become less intense and finally disappear.

◊ Celebrate the joyous feelings you have when you let go.

10

When You Choose Peace,
You Get Peace

"There is no way to peace, peace is the way."
—Source Unknown

Getting peace is a wonderful way for anything to turn out right. Choosing peace is a wonderful way to let it turn out right.

DETACHMENT

In June 1998, Sharon and I were spending two days of our vacation in Paris, staying near the Louvre Museum in an area familiar to us. We started a day trip to the countryside by going to the Metro and boarding the train. Just as the doors were closing, a slim girl about 4' 8" tall bumped into me and darted off the train. As she grabbed my wallet from my pants' pocket, I grabbed her tiny wrist and darted off the train with her, still holding on tightly. Her younger brother had distracted Sharon, but when she saw me dart off the train, she did too with little brother in the lead. I had read of the plan in travel magazines: the perpetrators take the wallet as the doors close and jump off the train before the targets figure out what's going on, so they are stuck on the departing train.

I recovered my wallet, looked at the four of us on the empty platform with the train disappearing into the tunnel, and assessed the situation. I chose peace. I wanted to take this girl to a police station to be booked. I had a strong grip encircling her wrist (not hurting her) and felt no anger toward her. Sharon and I thought we remembered where the neighborhood police station was, so we went up to the street level to look around. It wasn't where we thought it was. As we walked along the street, two plain-clothes men recognized the scene: Americans with pickpockets. They identified themselves as Metro police, and led us back into the Metro, four stops on the train, into the Metro police station. We learned of the girl's inches-thick dossier showing that she was a thirteen-year-old Bosnian refugee, sent out by her family to pick pockets, safe from prosecution by French law until she reached the age of 14. She was released.

How did I feel? In choosing peace, we elect not to have an emotional investment in the outcome, and the result was all right with me. I saw myself as giving the girl another reason to give up her life of crime before she turned 14: she wasn't skillful enough. Sharon saw that we kept her off the street for several hours.

I used force to get the peace I wanted. If I had been operating out of a different place, I could have let the girl go and chosen peace, too. Not able to lecture, coach, or advise her because of our language differences, I would have had to just let her go and choose peace. And I soon had an opportunity to do exactly that!

A week later in the middle of the afternoon, Sharon and I were sightseeing on one of the busiest streets in Milan, Italy. I was intent on photographing an interesting building across the street. I held the camera up to my eye and waited for a break in the traffic so the cars would not be in the picture. As I clicked the shutter, I was jostled by a small woman with a baby standing right in front of me. (At 6' 2" I could scarcely see her.) I grabbed her and yelled, "You took my wallet!" The wallet dropped to the ground, and I quickly picked it up. Apparently her accomplice was her mother, who pretended to be begging while jostling Sharon to keep her pre-occupied. In this case, we had only arrived in this city for the first time an hour or two before and were not ready to make the effort to take this trio to a police station. So we let them go and chose peace. Some of the passersby were concerned for our welfare and the pick-pocketing attempt; I wasn't.

When I look at these two events together, I see the same picture: my pocket was picked, I recovered the stolen item immediately, and I "captured" the thief—all while remaining detached from the outcome. I was satisfied with the French law requiring the authorities to release the girl and with my limitations in a strange city, which made me decide to release the women in Milan. Someone might say, "Why didn't you . . .?" or, "If that had been me, I would have . . ." I was content with the outcomes.

What would I do the next time? Choose peace, whatever that may entail. I might let my wallet go; "capture" the perpetrator, recover my wallet, and let her or him go; or "capture" the perpetrator and bring her or him to the authorities. When we choose peace, **they are all the same.**

PEACE IS A CHOICE

Peace is a way of being without experiencing uncomfortable feelings or fear. Choosing peace means making the choices that will bring you peace. In *A Course in Miracles*, a book devoted to teaching peace and love, we are taught to choose peace in every aspect of our lives, to make peace our primary goal. We have many choices in our lives: where we will live and work, what child care we will use, whether to seek a second job, who will be our friends, how we will develop personally, what to do on vacation, what to do for meals, how we will clothe ourselves and our family, with whom we will share our gifts. When we make all of our choices with peace as our goal, we will get peace.

A Peaceful Process

In 1986, I had to find a new job because the world oil picture had changed drastically in January of that year. Based on my experience and background, I looked for an opportunity to be a senior faculty member in chemical engineering. I had a deep sense of security: I would find the right job.

I responded to all the ads I could find and was offered one campus interview—a trip I took with Sharon. The faculty liked me but had not decided whether to hire someone with my background or someone from the environmental area. A few months after the interview, they still had not decided. Given those months to reflect, Sharon and I realized that we did not like the location. As a result, before receiving any other offer, I peacefully withdrew my application. Shortly after that, I turned down a possible offer because we thought the location would not offer us the opportunities for personal growth we were looking for. Two days later, we learned we were mistaken, so I asked for a job offer, received it, and accepted it. In each of those situations, we chose peace and got peace. The peace did not come from the job offer; the peace came from the process and the deep feeling or conviction (inner knowing) that it would turn out all right. I knew that if I didn't get a teaching position, I would go back to consulting and that would turn out right. These incidents occurred a couple of years before I knew *everything turns out right . . . when you let it.*

Choosing Not to Be Confused

After the job change, we were living in Charleston, WV. We were active in the Unity Church congregation, which we co-founded with a dozen others. In due time, the Board hired a minister and some issues arose that needed to be worked out. Some aspects of the ministry were going well and others were not. After a somewhat trying meeting, Sharon and I were driving home, discussing the events of the evening, and I said to her,

. . . when you let it

"I'm confused about the minister." I immediately said, "I can choose not to be confused." Reflecting on the issue, I realized my confusion stemmed from my desire to do something and not knowing what to do. Right after choosing not to be confused, the desire to do something evaporated, and I was at peace with the situation.

A BACK-UP PLAN

Another example of making choices that bring peace occurred when a friend of mine went to New York City with his wife to visit his sister and her husband and see a play. He had ordered four tickets online to be picked up at the box office. When they arrived early, they were told no tickets were being held for them. My friend knew the location of the seats they had been given but had no proof of his purchase. After a lengthy discussion, the manager said that just before curtain time he would look and if he found four empty seats where my friend said their seats were, they could take them. Disappointment!

While they waited for the outcome to unfold, after the initial surprise wore off, they enjoyed themselves discussing what they would do if they were unable to see the play. New York City offered many choices. They were at peace. At curtain time, the four seats they were waiting for were vacant. They went in and enjoyed the show, all the more for having chosen peace.

MONEY

Money decisions can be a source of stress. Choosing peace may mean deciding not to spend money. Sometimes we have our hearts set on something. It might be a special gift for a child or a spouse, dinner out, a new car, another car, a trip, a bigger house, new clothes, a new roof for the house, a digital camera, a new lawn, new outfits for the children, a big wedding for a daughter. We want very much to have that something, and the money is not available. In these days of easy credit, we can have

everything turns out right . . .

these things and not have to deal with the payment until later. But when we're asked to pay the bills, stress surfaces and peace evaporates. (The stress has been lying dormant all along, and the credit card statement brings it to life.) At this point, we can't avoid the financial pinch. Choosing peace here means taking responsibility for the original decision, recognizing our learning opportunity, deciding not to make any future financial commitments we can't afford, and seeing that *everything turns out right . . . when we let it.*

The decision not to make any future financial commitments may have to be made more than once. If the "learning experience" doesn't teach you what you need to learn, more opportunities will appear later. Perhaps you will be faced with a bigger expenditure: a new furnace or air conditioning unit on top of the expenses you've elected to make. This gives you another chance to choose peace. Maybe the best thing to do immediately is to correct the mistake: cancel the optional expense as soon as peace slips away, even if you must forfeit a deposit.

If a debt was not the result of your decision—maybe your spouse made the commitment—choosing peace means not taking responsibility for the outcome. You can help with the peaceful resolution without making the debt your problem. Without recriminations, pose the question, "How are we going to pay for this?" Saying "we" does not make it your problem, it merely acknowledges that your finances are held jointly. If they are not, "How are you going to pay for it?" is more appropriate.

We might realize in advance when we can't afford something we must have, such as a repair for the roof because it's leaking, or a car repair, because we need the car to drive to work, or medical attention. How can we choose peace when something like that happens? We know that worrying won't help (a small consolation but an important element in resolving the issue). Another thing we know is we have progressed this far, and, based on our history, we can expect to get through this too. Choosing peace here means you don't know how you will work it out, you are going to follow your guidance knowing you will get what you need (see Chapter 2), and you will work it out, perhaps in a way you can't even imagine. You may choose to repair the roof yourself, ask help from a neighbor, ask at work for the name of someone who might help, and explore many other alternatives. If you know *everything turns out right . . . when you let it*, you will be part of the solution.

CHILDREN

I have observed children acting up and aggravating their parents. Sometimes these behaviors mimic similar behaviors of the parents. This is not a scientific study but strongly suggests that if your relationship with your child is strained and you have difficulty choosing peace, the first place to look is within yourself. How are you contributing to this behavior? Perhaps the behavior is being modeled by someone other than you, but you don't have control over them. You can go within and look for the source. Possibly, you'll find it and discover that the behavior you don't like is your behavior. If that is the case, the first step in choosing peace with your child is to change your behavior. Keep in mind that the behaviors that challenge us the most are the ones that hold up a mirror in front of us so we can see more clearly who we are.

Sometimes our child, or someone who depends on us, may have his heart set on something, and the money is not available. Choosing peace includes telling the truth about the money, expressing your desire (if you have one) for him to have what he wants. If you just don't want him to have it, say so. If telling him you don't want him to have what he's asking for is a new experience for him, he might give you a negative response. That's okay. The important thing is not to take responsibility for his behavior. Don't say you're sorry you've made him cry, because you didn't. "I don't want you to be upset" is more appropriate and, with love and compassion, more accurate.

When my grandson was three years old, I took him and his nine-year-old cousin to the beach. At lunchtime, we had to leave the beach to go across the street for sandwiches and drinks. My grandson did not want to leave the beach and nothing I said could persuade him. So I picked him up and carried him gently, heading for the deli. He cried, getting increasingly loud. All the time we were crossing the beach, I was talking softly in his ear: "It's okay. We're just going for something to eat. We'll come back to the beach after we get our sandwiches. It's okay for you to cry. We'll be back on the beach soon." This continued until we reached the edge of the beach, at which point he quieted down and became peaceful. I had been at peace the whole time, not just on the outside but also with an inner peace and an occasional loss of patience, which I recovered by telling myself I was doing the right thing. When we were ready to cross the street, I put him down, we went to the deli, bought our sandwiches and drinks, and went back to our beach blanket and umbrella. My peace was a valuable contribution to his peace.

PUNISHMENTS AND REWARDS

To persuade a child to behave the way I want him to, do I want to threaten a punishment? No. Do I want to say, "If you do this thing I've told you not to do, I will give you the following punishment"? No. This puts the child in charge and offers him or her the opportunity to do exactly what I don't want, with my approval. Some parents trap themselves when they know the child may opt for the punishment instead of doing what he's told to do: they threaten a severe punishment, such as no TV for a year. When the child refuses to do what he's told, the parent is stuck. The parent won't mete out the punishment, and the child has disobeyed. The parent has not chosen peace.

Similarly, I don't want to offer a reward to a child for doing what I want him to. Here again, I would be proposing an agreement with the child allowing him or her not to do what I want, provided the child is willing to reject the reward. This is not the path to peace. Your response needs to provide an opportunity for the child to learn a different behavior. Tell the child what you

. . . when you let it

want done, not what you don't want. Take the time to show the child what you want every time a conflict arises; be relaxed, patient, and confident of the outcome. The things we do when we are not confident of the outcome—shouting, threatening, name-calling, judging—communicate clearly our fear of the child having his or her way, thus strengthening the child's resolve to prevail. Operate from the principle that *everything turns out right . . . when you let it*. Peace will come to you first. As you accept this peace and respond out of it, peace will come to the child. Finally, peace will come to the interactions between you and the child.

Over-defining the Problem

I know more than one person who appears to enjoy defining a problem over and over again without looking at a solution. Anything I suggest is immediately dismissed. When the problem has been defined exhaustively, another one is taken up for the same treatment. This person is in love with his or her problems and has not chosen peace.

If you find yourself dwelling on a problem with all its difficulties, intricacies, and ramifications, retelling it at every opportunity, and enjoying it all, take your behavior as a sign to choose peace. Look at the pay-off to you when you dwell on a problem. Meditate on the problem, let it go, and watch where your inner guidance takes you.

Looking at What Is

I have heard people angrily say, "I should have *known* he was going to do that." Or, "I *knew* he was going to do that." If so, why is the person surprised or angry? If we know or suspect someone is going to do something we don't like, standing back and just noticing it can be sufficient. One of the paths to peace is to look at what is, without judgment, interpretation, or naming it, as J. Krishnamurti has told us. When we choose peace, we are electing to be in the situation without frustration or anger.

We will not approve of or condone the behavior. To do so would mean giving up our personal values, a loss of integrity on our part. Our response to some action or inaction that makes us feel uncomfortable might be, "Okay, I see the way it is. Do I want to do anything to change the situation? What do I want to do? Forgive him? Talk peacefully to this person and suggest to him or her to act differently with no emotional investment in the outcome?" (Think to yourself, "I'm okay either way.")

Do I want to use force to get what I want? Do I want to manipulate anyone? Not when I'm choosing peace.

I live in Clearwater, FL, where we have many good roads, principally north-south arteries but also east-west connectors. They are sufficient to allow the traffic to move fairly smoothly but without the capacity to keep everyone moving at rush hour. We have a mixture of driver ages and styles and, in the winter, many people visiting from the north often drive at a leisurely pace. Other people weave in and out of three lanes to zoom ahead as many car lengths as possible. We also have people who race through an intersection after the light has been red for a few seconds. And other people, sharing the road with them, are experiencing "road rage"—frustration and anger at the behavior they are witnessing. I choose peace. I drive as fast as or maybe even faster than the flow of the traffic and without competing with the fast drivers for space. If someone wants to cut ahead of me in my lane, I slow down just a little and let him or her in. I know they won't be staying in front of me long, and I will soon be back where I was seconds ago. I make it okay. Sometimes when I think the driver is experiencing stress, I extend love and light to him. When I think the driver is having a good time, I may enjoy the fun he or she is having and wish the driver a safe journey. I get peace.

"I Don't Understand!"

A significant barrier to peace is the frustration expressed as, "I don't understand!" "Why is he doing that?" Or, "Why me?" The Bible speaks of the "Peace that passeth understanding," meaning we

. . . when you let it

don't have to understand what's going on to be at peace. I help by suggesting that the person whose behavior prompts the question, "Why is he doing that?" doesn't know the answer. If asked, he will in all likelihood have an **answer**, but not **the answer**, the deep answer, the truth. We might take years of work to know ourselves well enough to reach the point where we can speak the truth. When we ask the question "Why is she doing that?" it is safe to answer ourselves with "I don't know and she probably doesn't either." And it is okay. Clearly, struggling to understand and not being able to understand move us away from peace.

When we choose peace, we become observers. We give up any thought of diagnosing someone else's behavior or fixing it. We get peace, and we help when we're invited.

Noise That Might Disturb Our Peace

If noise is coming from a work project, such as someone mowing a lawn, building a road, etc., acknowledge in your head that someone is working nearby. You can go to sleep (choose peace) in the presence of noise. I've done it many times. Listen to the sounds. Are they coming from a loud party? Lying in your bed, join the party. Are they from a loud television? Listen to the program. By not resisting what you hear, you will release tensions and go to sleep. Many people have fallen asleep "watching" their favorite TV program. Their favorite show enables them to relax and go to sleep. *The Lullaby of Broadway* includes, " . . . the rumble of the subway trains, the rattle of the taxis . . ." These sounds are not part of everyone's lullaby but, if you love New York City and the sounds of the city, they may be part of yours. The sound is not bothering you; your relationship to the sound is.

Conflict Resolution

The cornerstone of my choosing peace in conflict resolution is the realization that no one is doing it to me. And we can safely assume everyone is doing the best he or she can. If someone is

everything turns out right . . .

not living peacefully, lovingly, and joyfully, I can assume they have some kind of handicap limiting their ability to do so. Anytime I'm upset, I can find the source within myself. Sometimes this is difficult to grasp.

A member of the church I was attending a few years ago asked me how to resolve an ongoing conflict with an aunt. She described the conflict and asked why her aunt was doing it to her. I told her, "One of the basic principles is that your aunt isn't creating the hurt and anguish; you are. Your aunt is just doing her thing, and it is safe to assume she is doing the best she can. I suggest you simply let go of the hurt." Apparently satisfied, she left. A few minutes later, she returned and asked, "But why is she doing it to me?"

How do we "simply let go of the hurt?" As I described in the previous chapter, letting go involves forgiving, in many cases over and over again. Each time the hurt appears—exhibited by tight muscles, headache, sadness, frustration or anger—we must forgive the person who we think has hurt us. To make the other person feel better? No, to bring peace to ourselves. Since the other person has not done anything to us, we are not forgiving any particular act or omission. We are just making that person okay in our minds and acknowledging that the other has not done anything to us. We are taking responsibility for how we feel, and we will forgive ourselves for our unloving behavior in the conflict. We will do this until reminders of the past hurt produce no effect except perhaps to manifest feelings of loving-kindness.

Then Peter came up and said to Him (Jesus), "Lord, how often shall my brother sin against me, and I forgive him? As many as seven times?" Jesus said to him, "I do not say to you seven times, but seventy times seven."[11]

. . . when you let it

We help ourselves when we keep in mind that the other person's behavior is not caused by us; it's caused by what the other person is thinking and feeling. We are not responsible for how the other feels. If we are verbally attacked, we can deflect the thrusts with, "I don't want you to be upset." If we are accused of making the other person feel bad, we can choose peace, "That's not my intention." As we do this each time the other person is upset, choosing peace becomes easier and easier.

In *A Course in Miracles, Workbook for Students*, we learn "I am never upset for the reason I think."[12] Our primary source of upset is feeling unloved, unappreciated, "less than." This is true for the other person, too. The anger and upset we see is described in *A Course in Miracles* as *a call for love*. What that person needs is love and reassurance, not to be made wrong. If we make the other person wrong, we can expect a vigorous defense and counterattack.

Win-Win

One of the hallmarks of peaceful conflict resolution is the desire for the other person to win. It is based on *satyagraha* (looking for truth), the underlying principle in Mohandas Gandhi's peace efforts. "Look for the truth in the other person's position." Together, seek a solution enabling both sides to have what they want. The process is not so much a negotiation as it is a co-operative search for a creative solution. If the conflict is over how big a piece of pie each person will get, the resolution might be to make a bigger pie. And the entire process is peaceful.

M. Gandhi also demonstrated that choosing peace does not mean succumbing to the will of others. M. Gandhi was aggressive in his campaign; he was waging peace. He was peacefully calling attention to injustices in India, with the purpose of ridding the country of British colonial rule. The British had placed a tax on salt, and Gandhi led his followers to the sea where they made salt from the seawater. The British saw his activities as defying the law, and he saw them as peacefully calling attention to British oppression, taxing poor people for one of the staples of their diet.

The opposite of waging peace is angering, which denotes choosing to be angry. One of the members of our original *A Course in Miracles* study group used the word "angering" to underscore that being angry is a choice.[13] Watching my personal reaction to challenging situations, I see clearly that I am choosing between waging peace and angering. I usually choose to wage peace but sometimes I allow myself to anger. Sooner or later, I'm aware that my anger is not a result of the situation or the other person. I realize it's a result of my not choosing peace, and I let go as quickly as I can.

Why do we get angry? For many of us and many situations, it is a defensive step to intimidate the other person, make him or her feel wrong or guilty, and thereby get what we want. Our angry feelings are most likely to well up when an area in which we feel insecure is threatened. For example, I am careful about spending my money and often choose not to spend money on things others are buying or doing; not spending money is an area of sensitivity for me. If a conflict arises with someone who accuses me of being a cheapskate and a penny pincher, I may become upset and angry. I could attack my accuser by making some counter-accusations, or choose peace and simply explain that I work hard for my money and always want to be careful how I spend it. On the other hand, if I am accused of being a thief and a cheat, my reaction will be unemotional (peaceful) because I know I am neither.

Conflict seems to be a particularly difficult arena in which to choose peace. You must start with the idea that non-violent conflict is all right; it is based simply on different points of view and different interests. Conflict seems inevitable in everyday life; how you resolve it is what matters. Choosing peace means looking at "what is" and responding with integrity. Suppose you find a situation that doesn't meet your expectations. Now what do

. . . when you let it

you want to do? What is the loving thing to do? Can you do it? Do you want to do it? Make the choice that will bring you peace, and you will get peace. Make the choice with love.

Our relationships provide many opportunities to choose peace. Spouses, children, parents, other relatives, significant others, friends, co-workers, church members, club members, fellow volunteers, service people, all have the potential to provide us with opportunities to choose between peace and anger.

SPOUSES

Your relationship with your spouse or significant other provides an excellent opportunity to wage peace. Spouses make many decisions affecting each other. They are called upon to work together; to play together; often to raise children together; to create intimacy; to support each other physically, emotionally, spiritually, and financially; to give each other space; and, to let each one have a life of his and her own. To be close and not suffocating. To be helpful and not controlling. To be loving and not domineering. In order to wage peace, be aware that all of these aspects of a spousal relationship, and more, are arenas for waging peace. If you let go of your preferences (Chapter 9) as core values, you will eliminate many points of friction and conflict. Your preferences won't matter. And after letting go of them, you will more easily be able to wage peace in the areas left.

Waging peace means choosing, over and over again, to do the kind, giving, and helpful thing. After many years of waging peace, Sharon and I are sufficiently skilled at this so that in the middle of a conflict, we will often switch sides. As a result, the decision is a peaceful one because we both have expressed the appropriateness of it.

If the idea of doing "the kind, giving, and helpful thing" doesn't appeal to you, ask yourself, "Why not? What am I afraid of?" Being seen as weak? Being dominated? Taken advantage of? These are serious issues. Are you afraid of your spouse? Maybe not. Maybe you have some old fears of being perceived as weak that you must

everything turns out right . . .

release before you can wage peace. The place to start your peace campaign is by searching within to find what is holding you back from being a kind, generous, helpful spouse. Listening to your inner guidance and acting on it will show you the way.

Your waging peace must be based on love, not fear. If you are afraid of your spouse, a different campaign is required. Your path to peace may be to a therapist, a counselor, a minister, a trusted friend or relative, someone who can help you escape from the threatening environment. Listen to your inner guidance regarding what steps to take. By choosing peace, you will begin to see the way out and you will get peace.

A friend of mine who is also a business associate needed to go with his wife to visit her sister who was seriously ill. The trip was 500 miles by car to a city beyond Columbus, Ohio, with my friend driving. When they reached Columbus, my friend decided to choose the route around the city instead of through it—a greater distance but quicker, he figured. His wife thought the more direct route would have been better and became unhappy with her husband and his choice. She was anxious to see her sister and didn't want to take any more time to reach her than was absolutely necessary. In returning, he went through Columbus instead of around it and the trip was slow. When he told me this story a few days later, I asked him, "Did you point this out to your wife?"

He replied, "No, I didn't because I didn't want to upset her." He didn't want to make her wrong. He had chosen peace and received peace. If we do this every day, we will come to expect peace and recognize the peaceful choices we can make.

I have lived in a contentious environment and in a peaceful one. The peaceful one is better. What makes the difference? Being aware of the choice not to argue; noticing that my inclination to argue is not because of the merits of the situation but simply because I'm inclined to argue at that moment, and I don't need to; seeing the truth in my spouse's position; being as overtly supportive of my spouse as I can be; and accepting the outcome when I don't get my way, especially when I think I have a better way or a better idea.

. . . when you let it

Consistency

In *Love is Letting Go of Fear*, Gerald G. Jampolsky writes, "Sometimes we put more value in predicting and controlling than in having peace of mind."[14] He goes on to say, "To have inner peace, we need to be consistent in having peace of mind as our single goal."

Suppose someone makes a decision you don't like. If you have peace of mind as your single goal, you will not put any energy into making whoever made the decision wrong. Be part of the solution; choose peace. Put a big chapter heading on this episode, "<Your name> Learns to Choose Peace."

Welcome the opportunity to do this. We grow slowly without real-life interactions and challenges. We benefit from people who say and do abrasive things. The grinding stone removes the rough edges from the steel blade, and we may be smoothed in the same way. To become completely transformed we will need to do more than read a book, attend a conference, or talk to a counselor. Usually, the best we can do for ourselves is to allow ourselves to be pointed in another direction and " . . . be consistent in having peace of mind as our single goal." Every action we take or don't take, every challenge, every conflict, every conversation, every personal encounter, every nightly newscast, every sports event, and every thought give us the opportunity to be consistent in having peace of mind as our single goal. We can do it.

Prayer of St. Francis[15]

Sometimes we hear, "<someone> has the patience of a saint." The following is advice from St. Francis of Assisi on how we can achieve that level of peace.

> Lord, make me an instrument of thy peace.
> Where there is hatred, let me sow love;
> Where there is injury, pardon;

everything turns out right . . .

Where there is doubt, faith;
Where there is despair, hope;
Where there is darkness, light;
Where there is sadness, joy;

O divine Master, grant that I may not so much seek
To be consoled as to console,
To be understood as to understand,
To be loved as to love;
For it is in giving that we receive;
It is in pardoning that we are pardoned;
It is in dying [to self] that we are born to eternal life.

We are committing to sow love, pardon (forgiveness), faith, hope, light, and joy as well as to be consoling, understanding, and loving. We do this because it is in giving that we receive. In making these choices for peace, we will get peace.

And we can help ourselves by keeping in mind the opening line of The Peace Song, *"Let there be peace on earth and let it begin with me."*[16]

. . . when you let it

Summary

◈ When you choose peace, you get peace.

◈ The behaviors that challenge us the most are the ones mirroring our own.

◈ Be part of the solution.

◈ In relating to children, promises of rewards and threats of punishment put the child in charge and take away your peace.

◈ Have no emotional investment in the outcome of any of your endeavors.

◈ If you are upset, find the source within yourself.

◈ Waging peace is repeatedly choosing to do the kind, loving, giving, helpful thing.

◈ All of our relationships provide excellent opportunities to choose peace.

11

Live Each Day
as if It Were Your First

"'Tis well an old age is out, and time to begin a new."
—John Dryden

I have heard the advice to "Live each day as if it were your last" a few times, and it never appealed to me. It has an unsatisfactory note of finality. Furthermore, if this were truly my last day, I would gather my family and friends around me in order to enjoy each other one last time. If this were truly my last day, I could afford to do that. If not, I have a lot of things to do. I would be delighted to spend the day, any day, sitting around with family and friends, but that's not the way I'm going to live each day. That's not how they're going to live each day either.

The people who say, "Live each day as if it were your last," want us to be more focused, more intense, more in a hurry to do things. That's not how I want to live my life. ". . . as if it were your last" is not in keeping with the basic principle *everything turns out right . . . when you let it.*

SOMETHING SPECIAL

What makes our first day special? It carries no memory, no sense of future—we have no past to project into the future—we see the world anew. We are "letting it" every moment.

I was in the U. S. Army stationed in a little town on Tokyo Bay just south of Yokohama from the summer of 1953 to the spring of 1954. By traveling on some weekends as well as taking day trips to Tokyo and enjoying the local sights, I saw a lot of exotic Asian faces, natural beauty, Shinto shrines and temples, farms on terraced hillsides, snowcapped Mt. Fuji (as shown in travel ads), sub-compact cars, and Japanese language signs and billboards. I also ate local foods with new flavors and heard totally unfamiliar music streaming from loudspeakers mounted on light poles along the streets. I smelled unusual perfumes, pomades, and flowering trees. I listened to the slurping of tea and imitated it as well as I could in order to be a polite guest at a Tea Ceremony. While not indoctrinated, before leaving I was becoming acculturated to Japanese ways.

Upon returning home to the States in early July, everything looked new. I saw different people, natural beauty, churches and synagogues, farms on the flatlands of New Jersey, no mountains in sight, and English language signs and billboards. Before going into the Army, I had spent the previous eleven years in New Jersey, and now I was back. Everything was bright, colorful, standing out like *bas-relief,* and a little like a 3-D movie. I was excited, not only to be discharged from the Army but also to be seeing all this for the first time. I didn't remember feeling this way before. What had happened? I had left New Jersey less than a year before and now everything had changed. What exactly had changed? I had. I was looking with fresh eyes and seeing details I had never seen before. I was filled with wonder.

In the *Wizard of Oz*, when Dorothy says to Toto, "I have a feeling we're not in Kansas anymore," she speaks with awe. I felt a lot like Dorothy when I returned.

You feel a sense of wonder when you live each day as if it were your first. If you have bought a new vehicle sometime in your life, you may have experienced this feeling. You have completed the purchase, the temporary tags are on, and you drive away from the dealer's showroom. You are exhilarated. You are fully alive, everything looks wonderful, and you are handling the car, the truck, or the SUV with ease. You may look for an open road or an Interstate to let loose a little. You're looking at the dashboard with its new arrangement of indicators and controls; you're also looking at the surrounding buildings and countryside and seeing them as if for the first time. You have no worries about romance, family, job, finances, home repairs, or health. If your vehicle moves a little close to another one, you might worry briefly about scratching it before you get home. You recognize the worry as old fearful thinking, so you let the thought go and return to the marvelous experience of now. This entire driving episode is like living each day as if it were your first.

Living each day as if it were your first is different from functioning in some sort of trance. Many people have had the experience of driving without being aware of their surroundings. On occasion, I have driven ten miles or more and suddenly realized I have not "seen" anything; I had just awakened from a trance. My car and I were on some kind of auto-pilot. This state has usually been induced by deep thought and seems to be unrelated to drowsiness. The experience of driving the vehicle away from the dealer's showroom, as described above, is different. The feelings come from heightened awareness, not a trance.

Living each day as if it were your first means living without guilt or baggage from the past and without fear of the future. You have a clean slate. You are living without judgment because you have nothing to compare with what you're experiencing.

KEEPING YOUR SKILLS

Living each day as if it were your first has two parts: skills and emotions. Notice you can live this way without losing your skills. You need to hold on to your everyday skills such as driving, cooking, and work skills. You will find no inconsistency between having "no memory" and being able to drive. They belong to different parts of your awareness. You do many things by rote and, by living each day as if it were your first, you can bring those skills to your awareness and make them fully available to you in everyday life.

We have skills deeply rooted in our memories, skills such as riding a bike. "It's just like riding a bike" is a metaphor for the ease of using a skill we have not employed in a long time. If you once rode a bike comfortably and get on a bike ten years later, in minutes (or less), you will be riding with essentially the same comfort level as before. You might not have the strength you had before, but you will have the skill; maintaining your balance— the key skill for novices—will come to you easily.

You know the mechanics of living, and you will not lose these skills. You know the *procedures* you use in doing your job, in taking care of your children and the place you live, in driving, in golfing, in cooking, in playing tennis, in singing, in dancing, in swimming, in repairing autos, in fishing, and in everything else you use to live your life. You will not lose these. Just for now, focus on the purely mechanical aspect of those activities, free from emotional involvement. If negative or fearful thoughts come up, put them aside. If positive thoughts come up, look at them, and let them go.

SETTING ASIDE YOUR EMOTIONS

You might wonder, "How can I set aside my emotions? They just happen! I don't control them." Each of our emotional experiences, wonderful or not, is preceded by a thought triggering the emotion. To set aside your emotional responses, you need to

. . . when you let it

replace any thought rooted in yesterday's experience of yourself or others in your life. You need to replace it with openness to a new awareness. When you strip away all of the feelings associated with everyday tasks, you will reduce them to just a series of cut-and-dried steps you know well, as well as you know how to ride a bicycle or to recite the alphabet. Now as you do your everyday tasks, you will have no question of "Why am I doing this?", or "I hope this turns out to be a good dinner," "This is a boring job," or "Getting away for a day of fishing is great." The terms *good, boring,* and *great* are judgments made about these activities; the judgments are rooted in the past. When you live each day as if it were your first, you will have no past experiences to draw upon.

Notice what feelings remain. I expect you feel disconnected. Without your emotional involvement in what you are doing, your life may seem empty, sterile, unsatisfying. You might be in an emotional vacuum. However, the emotional part of your life will change when you live each day as if it were your first. What are you disconnected from? Your feelings of inadequacy in parenting and job performance perhaps? Frustration with your skills in golfing, in cooking, in playing tennis, in singing, in dancing, in swimming, in repairing autos, and in fishing? Fear of being left out, falling behind, or not being loved? Feelings of lack of time, money, beauty, or health, of not being okay or appreciated? You might also feel disconnected from joy, love, and a sense of the Divine, but you will reconnect with them. You will reconnect with them because, when feelings of inadequacy, frustration, fear, and lack are gone and an emotional vacuum has been created inside you, love, which is your natural state, will fill you.

When you live each day as if it were your first, all of the uncomfortable feelings fade away. Whatever you are doing, you will be calling on your Inner Knowing, the place where you've stored your ability to ride a bike, recite the alphabet, do your job, change a diaper, and everything else you know how to do. You will have suspended judgment about how you

everything turns out right . . .

are doing. When you are living in the present, your mind will not be cluttered. You will not be pre-occupied with what you did or didn't do in the past, or what you want to do tomorrow or the next day. You'll be more relaxed doing what you're doing and not concerned about the outcome. Letting go of the past and the future means you will be giving your full attention to right now, meditating, exercising, or using your skills just for their own sake. And, whatever you're doing, you will be more successful than before.

LIVING YOUR FIRST DAY (EVERY DAY)

You're at the leading edge of your life. You are not limited by what you did or didn't do in the past. You are open to the possibilities life has to offer.

One of the themes of *A Course in Miracles* is that we are co-creators with God, that is, co-creators of our lives. By living each day as if it were our first, we have this wonderful opportunity to start fresh every day. Each one is all new. We will cherish our everyday experiences because they are all new.

I recently had the opportunity to speak with a 93-year-old woman who had just been named Volunteer of the Month. I told her she made 93 look good. With a lot of sincerity, she leaned forward speaking softly as if she were sharing a secret and replied, "Life is for living." By living in the present, we are focusing on living, co-creating new experiences for whatever purposes we have.

When you are living as if it were your first day, you are much more open to your inner guidance. You will have no tapes in your head persistently telling you what to do and what not to do. Instead, you want and will ask for inner guidance: "What am I to do?" and "What am I supposed to be learning from this?" Without any tapes, your uncluttered mind is more aware of the inner guidance available to you. You make choices leading you to a richer, more loving and more fulfilling life.

You will be living life as a whole rather than as an assembly of parts. The parts of your life have labels: parent; husband; wife;

. . . when you let it

son; daughter; worker; homemaker; deacon; board member; golfer; and many others denoting your position in family life, social life, work life, church life, etc. When you're living at the leading edge, you will be beyond these labels. You will still have the family, friends, jobs, church, etc. you had before. But they will be vehicles for you to extend love and thereby experience more love yourself. What does this have to do with living each day as if it were your first? By doing so, you melt the barriers to experiencing yourself as a totally loving person. These barriers include the desire to control; the fear of being controlled; the fear of lack of time, money, or love; and the fear of not being okay. All of these fears separate you internally; without them, you will be living a whole life. And you won't have to give them up one by one. When you live each day as if it were your first, your fears will fade away.

MOVING ON

Each day is an opportunity for transformation. Every thought rooted in the past takes away our ability to live in the present. Every thought projected into the future does the same. Looking into the past—whether ten minutes, ten weeks or ten years ago—does not hurt as long as you look without anger, guilt, regrets, or other negative feelings. Looking into the future without fear, anxiety, or apprehension does not hurt either. But even these seemingly innocuous diversions do take away your ability to live in the present where you are on the leading edge of your life. Each time you are pulled away from the present, center yourself again by choosing to focus on the here and now.

Am I saying that planning the activities of tomorrow, next week, or next year is undesirable? No, just that planning will take you away from living in the present. By living today as if it were your first without planning, you open yourself up to the possibility of living a fully spontaneous life, letting others do the planning, watching what unfolds for you. If you don't like what has been planned for you, you will choose to do something else.

everything turns out right . . .

You will avoid the inherent limitations of living the planned life, because it tends to pull you away from co-creating your life with God and the Universe.

How will you meet your responsibilities? Getting to work on time? Picking up the children? As you move into the spontaneous life, you'll know what to do and you'll do it.

You cannot expect to abruptly switch from a busy, planned-down-to-the-minute life to a totally spontaneous life. Take that as a goal. You might want to plan your wedding, your parenthood, your children's education, your career, your retirement, and your funeral. And, as you continue to make plans, fewer of them perhaps, you will want to make sure you don't identify too closely with the plan. You will be able to let go when the plan is not working for you.

"Better" vs. Authentic

I expect you want to live a better life. The details will vary widely from reader to reader: better future for your children, more financial security, greater spirituality, more fun, closer connection to God, more loving relationships, improved health, and many others. Each of these requires you to feel some sense of lack. If you live each day as if it were your first, that sense of lack disappears. You will have nothing to compare your experience to. You will, however, have the opportunity to live an authentic life. Out on the leading edge, you will have integrity (wholeness), love, patience, forgiveness, compassion, gratitude, and all the other attributes of an authentic life. This is the gift of living in the present.

Handling New Situations

You might find the unfamiliar threatening. In particular, handling some kinds of new situations might be difficult. Perhaps you don't accept a new situation as another adventure but only as anxiety-producing or even frightening. When you live each

. . . when you let it

day as if it were your first, you will encounter no "new situations." Without previous experiences as references, you will see no differences. Perhaps a new situation calls for skills you don't have. They could be social, technical, professional, or other. Living in the here and now, you will either acquire them or choose not to perform the task. You will not feel threatened or inadequate. You have no basis for doing so.

A Fresh Look

When you live each day as if it were your first, you have an opportunity to absorb what you're seeing and experiencing in a different way. When you're out on the leading edge, you will find you can safely assume that all the people you are aware of— loved ones, friends, neighbors, politicians, co-workers, church members, public figures, service personnel, club members—are doing the best they can. You will see some of them struggling with their demons, breaking the law, breaking public trust, hurting others in a variety of ways, and you will know they will benefit from your compassion and forgiveness. Living in the present, you will recognize them as your brothers and sisters, and you will extend love to them. You will also realize many of the people you encounter are generous, compassionate, loving, forgiving, and kind, and you will enjoy the gifts they share with the world. You will love them; all of them are your brothers and sisters too.

Living One Day as if It Were Your First

This is a different experience and quite extraordinary. To provide some anchor points, we will look at what can happen when you make this choice. Throughout the day, you will always be able to go within, relying on Inner Knowing to guide you.

Waking up. If you live with loved ones, you will see them for the first time. If you're alone, you can look in the mirror and see yourself for the first time. Regardless of who you see, that person will simply be that person. He or she will not look either good or frazzled. Just feel the love.

At work. You will choose to do the work to be done. You will not resist because you have no way to judge the value of the work. You won't be given "dumb" assignments. You won't say, "I don't understand why . . . " You will meet a broad mixture of people. Some will be fearful, warning of dire outcomes, critical, complaining, blaming. Others will be loving, cheerful, warm, encouraging to others. You will extend love to them all.

At lunch. You will enjoy your lunch, whatever you are eating. Instinctively you will avoid the foods you are allergic to or your body will have let go of the allergies. (The evidence for the possibility of letting go of your allergies comes from people with multiple personalities. One personality will have certain allergies and the others—with the same body, of course—will not have those allergies. See, for example, Michael Talbot's, *The Holographic Universe,* HarperPerennial, pages 97-100 (1992). When I learned about this, I realized how much I don't know about how everything works.)

Going home. What radio station do you want to play? What audio tape? Book on tape? Inspirational tape? What CD? The choice doesn't matter, for they're all new to you. You may prefer silence.

Being at home alone. You may have had the experience of seeing a movie for a second time or rereading a book and discovering things you missed before. This can happen the third time around as well. I have read *A Course in Miracles* three times and have learned a lot each time. A friend recently told me she had seen the movie Simon Burch ten times and had seen something more each time. Others have read the Bible many times with deepening understanding. These examples indicate that, even when you are not living each day as if it were your first, you can still re-experience something as "new," interesting, even exciting. When we are living in the present, all of our experiences will be that way. What are you drawn to do at home alone? Read? Get back to a hobby? Play the piano? Pay bills? Make home repairs?

. . . when you let it

Do laundry? Walk the dog? Do whatever you choose. You will do what you choose without resistance. You will get great pleasure from doing so. And your life will flow.

Being at home with people you love. Being a loving person is your nature. Being at home with people you love provides a wonderful opportunity to manifest and express your love in all of your interactions with them. Nothing is carried over from past differences, disagreements, or arguments, nothing to be in the way of loving conversations. So you enjoy your activities, welcoming the exchanges you have with the people you love.

Reconnecting with Transcendent Love

When you live each day as if it were your first, the negative emotions have faded away. When you sense the emotional vacuum, let love in to fill the void. The love is nearby waiting to be invited in. It is love for yourself and who you are, for what you are doing, for all the people you encounter, for life itself. The love coming to you this way is natural, without longing, without expectations, without conditions. We can extend this love to everyone and everything in our lives without longing, without expectations, without conditions. In fact, if we extend love that way, we will experience it ourselves. As soon as we start living as if it were our first day, we will experience this Love, transcendent love.

Extending love to everyone you encounter is a consequence of living today as if it were your first. Love, loving kindness, and compassion are our natural states; when we strip away the negativity, apprehension, and fear, we are left with love. Without the past to hold us back and without fear of the future, we are not only free to act lovingly towards each one we meet, we will actually act that way.

Being with people for whom you do not have loving feelings. Picture in your mind a person you find irritating, a pain in the neck, a troublemaker. Now let go of all memories of that person and just keep the picture in mind. If negative feelings come up, trace them to their sources, to memories of past hurts, perhaps, and let them go. Keep the picture of the troublemaker in your mind and let go of any past hurts. As you do this, you are moving closer to relating to that person as if it were your first encounter, closer to living this day as if it were your first. As you repeat this process again and again, perhaps over a period of weeks or months, you will more easily picture this person without negative emotions coming up for you. As you make your transition away from experiencing this person as irritating, a pain in the neck, a troublemaker, you will let go of all of your past history with this person, and Divine Love will creep into your consciousness. You will begin to realize that the flaws you have seen so clearly call for your compassion and love. You will see that without the burden of past problems, you can give yourself permission to be compassionate and loving.

Now extend this to everyone you know, to every irritant no matter how small. Start from the beginning, deliberately letting go of the negative feelings by knowing their roots are in the past. Continue this process with each person as negative feelings come up for you. Develop the habit of seeing each person with new eyes. Realize that all your negative feelings are rooted in the past; you can let go of all of them.

When you seem to have completed this process with anyone, the next time you meet that person, you will have loving feelings, perhaps mixed with the old negative feelings. The person may be exhibiting the very behavior that has alienated you in the past. See that Love, through you, is available to heal your relationship. See the person as your child, regardless of age, to be cared for in a loving way. See that the child brings to this moment a lifetime of experiences including hurts and disappointments. See that this child is holding on to them and has not chosen to live this day as if it were its first. See that you have a wonderful opportunity to demonstrate the power of doing just that. See that loving this child does not condone its behavior. See that extending love in any situation is a show of strength, inner strength, not weakness. Allow Love to operate in and through you by living each day as if it were your first.

. . . when you let it

Summary

- ◈ Live without feelings from the past and without anticipation of the future; be in the Now.

- ◈ Develop the habit of seeing each person and situation with new eyes.

- ◈ When you let go of the past and fully embrace the present, you will live with heightened awareness.

- ◈ Negative feelings will be replaced by love, without longing, expectations or conditions.

- ◈ You will be co-creating with God.

12

When You Let Go, You Feel Joy

"Most people are about as happy as they make up their minds to be."
—Abraham Lincoln

This takes us one step beyond the basic principle, beyond "turning out right" to turning out joyous. After you have let go of the end of your rope, your over-commitments, your emotional investment in the outcome of things you can't control, after you've let go of all of these, just watch, watch your life like a movie. Your life is a movie and you're the main character. You're this wonderful, sympathetic, lovable character. Just watch the movie because you're the star. The movie has its ups and downs; it's a wonderful story and you can learn so much by just watching it, by letting go of all judgment throughout. Feel the joy of it.

In addition to being the star, here are some other ways you will be, as part of feeling joy:

Fully alive in your everyday experiences.

Open.

At peace.

Confident.

Adventuresome.

Aware of your oneness with God and all living things.

How can you let go and feel the joy? Below is a list of some attributes you might want to let go of so you do feel the joy. You have 37 to choose from, so see if you can find one for yourself. If you find more than one to let go of, choose the one you think would bring you the most joy, just one. Focus on just that one. Meditate on it. Notice how you feel when you release the unwanted part of yourself. See if the change provides a good fit with who you are. Create an image of yourself as you will be after you have let go of that particular attribute. Hold onto that image and be prepared to bring it to your consciousness whenever you would like its support and guidance. Feel the joy of it.

Notice that letting go of an attribute involves a different way of being. To let go of hurts, for example, we need to be forgiving. And as we become forgiving, we will be letting go of other attributes such as blame, slights, and judgment. This letting go

TO LET GO OF THESE:	BE THIS WAY:	AND THEN:
Let go of guilt.	Be authentic.	*Feel joy.*
Let go of hurts.	Be forgiving.	*Feel joy.*
Let go of blame.	Be forgiving.	*Feel joy.*
Let go of slights.	Be forgiving.	*Feel joy.*
Let go of control.	Be relaxed.	*Feel joy.*
Let go of "I can't."	Be authentic.	*Feel joy.*
Let go of injustice.	Be compassionate.	*Feel joy.*
Let go of inferiority.	Be authentic.	*Feel joy.*
Let go of judgment.	Be forgiving.	*Feel joy.*

To Let Go of These:	Be This Way:	And Then:
Let go of lost loves.	Be loving.	*Feel joy.*
Let go of schedules.	Be relaxed.	*Feel joy.*
Let go of resistance.	Be loving.	*Feel joy.*
Let go of superiority.	Be authentic.	*Feel joy.*
Let go of being right.	Be authentic.	*Feel joy.*
Let go of aggression.	Be loving.	*Feel joy.*
Let go of resentment.	Be forgiving.	*Feel joy.*
Let go of doing more.	Be okay with yourself.	*Feel joy.*
Let go of getting even.	Be forgiving.	*Feel joy.*
Let go of looking good.	Be authentic.	*Feel joy.*
Let go of weight issues.	Be okay with yourself.	*Feel joy.*
Let go of defensiveness.	Be loving.	*Feel joy.*
Let go of the daily news.	Be compassionate.	*Feel joy.*
Let go of co-dependence.	Be authentic.	*Feel joy.*
Let go of acquisitiveness.	Be okay with yourself.	*Feel joy.*
Let go of financial issues.	Be okay with yourself.	*Feel joy.*
Let go of power struggles.	Be compassionate.	*Feel joy.*
Let go of competitiveness.	Be cooperative.	*Feel joy.*
Let go of having your way.	Be cooperative.	*Feel joy.*

everything turns out right . . .

To Let Go of These:	Be This Way:	And Then:
Let go of your health issues.	Be okay with yourself.	*Feel joy.*
Let go of not having enough.	Be okay with yourself.	*Feel joy.*
Let go of figuring out your life.	Be relaxed.	*Feel joy.*
Let go of the drama in your life.	Be authentic.	*Feel joy.*
Let go of "I'm not good enough."	Be authentic.	*Feel joy.*
Let go of emotional investment in outcomes.	Be okay with yourself.	*Feel joy.*
Let go of dependence on the opinions of others.	Be authentic	*Feel joy.*
Let go of health issues of your loved ones, relatives, friends, and co-workers.	Be loving.	*Feel joy.*
Let go of drama in the lives of your loved ones, relatives, friends, and co-workers.	Be loving.	*Feel joy.*

requires a new way of being, which in turn allows us to release at least one other attribute . . . for free!

Letting go is somewhat like learning to use a computer. In each case, the beginners need to be assured that they can't ruin anything. Letting go of the attribute of your choice will not ruin anything. You will be lighter, stronger, happier, more loving, just from letting go of the one thing you have chosen as the greatest barrier to having more joy in your life.

Developing a new way of being requires the same kind of patience and perseverance we use to acquire any skill. Realize the mistakes we make are only reminders we have not completely embraced the new way of being. Mistakes are okay; we'll have

. . . when you let it

other chances. A year after realizing I was on a spiritual path, I was visiting with a group of supportive friends. I was enjoying my new way of being, but had to admit I was only now where I thought I was six months earlier. I laughed and my friends laughed with me because they had had the same experience.

BE AUTHENTIC

To be authentic, or real, is to behave in accord with who you are. I find a lot of evidence indicating we are spiritual beings having physical experiences and not the other way around. The evidence for this comes to us from the many reports of near-death experiences and from people on the other side who have crossed over and communicated back through psychic mediums. If you don't accept this evidence, you will still benefit greatly from being authentic and will need to know who you are.

Your essential facts are simply that you are whole, perfect, and complete. To be authentic, you must live out of your awareness of the validity of this for you. And this is without regard to any physical, mental, or emotional characteristics you may exhibit, such as your age, IQ, agility, vision, hearing, beauty, strength, talent, charisma, weight, addictions, ability to see auras, or success in your vocation or avocation. How could this be? It is because you are a spiritual being, not a collection of attributes.

"We are not human beings in search of a spiritual experience. We are spiritual beings immersed in a human experience." — Pierre Teilhard de Chardin.

everything turns out right . . .

Shakespeare has told us, "All the world's a stage and all the men and women merely players." We have chosen our parts. When James Earl Jones played the part of Othello, he did not become a murderer but he did experience what it was like to be one. When it was over, he went back to real life and to being the person he was before he took on his stage role. Our real selves, our spiritual selves, do the same. We come to earth to have the experience of being in our physical bodies and to create loving expressions of our physical selves. Some choose roles that seem to us to be difficult and demanding, while others apparently have an easy time here on Earth. Our purposes are all the same: we are in this play we call "Life" to use our unique roles to create loving expressions of who we are. I believe that when we are listening to the Director of this play—Holy Spirit, our inner guidance, or the Voice for God—we are indeed co-creators with God. This may not seem to be who you are at this time. That's all right. Just know you are whole, complete, and perfect; the rest will come.

You have made mistakes. Perhaps you regret some of them deeply. That doesn't change the fact that you are whole, complete, and perfect. Those feelings of being a bad person we call *guilt* have no place in your authentic emotional palette. The things you do out of guilt you could choose to do out of love, or you could choose not to do them. In taking care of an elderly parent or a neglected child, thinking of someone who has passed on, or buying expensive gifts, you can act out of love instead of guilt. And when you are authentic, you will not be saying yes when you want to say no. You will live out of your wholeness. And you will feel joy.

When you are authentic, you will not have a false sense of inadequacy. The thought, *"I can't"* is largely based on fear of failure, and you will set the thought aside. In its place, you will know "If at first you don't succeed, relax and you will" is true for you.

My cousin, Robert, was the most loving person I have known. He was diagnosed as a Down's Syndrome baby and had

. . . when you let it

the symptoms associated with that diagnosis. This was in the 1930s, before much was known about how to enable these children and adults to fully realize themselves. Nevertheless, Robert was authentic. He expressed love more easily than anyone in the family and was a model for me, although many years elapsed before I even began to express love the way he did. Sometimes he was upset or angry, and sometimes he was ill. Some people, including family members, were put off by Robert's different appearance, but Robert seemed to accept that. His behavior was authentic, as if he knew that he was whole, complete, and perfect. He learned, too. His sister taught him reading and writing—enough to have simple correspondence with relatives—and the arithmetic he used to keep score in games. And he also learned the skills needed to take care of others less able than he. In all of this, he was blessed with the love of his mother and sister. I don't know what the spirit who came here as Robert had in mind but, from my earthbound point of view, it was a great experience for many people in his life.

When you live authentically, you have no sense of *inferiority* or *superiority*. If the thought, "I'm not good enough" enters your mind, allow it to float away. Instead of trying to prove you are *right*, recognize the limits of your knowledge and look for the truth in all situations. If the truth coincides with your opinion, let it go; be content to know the truth. Manipulating any situation to *look good* is the antithesis of living authentically. You don't have to *convince* anyone you're okay; you are okay. If you think of *looking good* in terms of the clothing you wear and your appearance, keep in mind that life is not a costume party. And you can enjoy the authentic dress of people here at home, including yourself, and around the world.

When you live authentically, you let go of the *drama* in your life and the lives of the people around you. You do not get caught up in the anxiety, fear, judgment, and anger making up the drama. You realize everything is okay. You accept the good that comes to you and are grateful. You share the good and the news of the good with the others in your life. When people come to you with physical, emotional, mental, and spiritual problems, you extend love to them and to the ones they are involved with. And if at times you don't love the characters in your play, you can love the actors who are creating those parts, the spiritual beings who reside in the bodies you know.

When you live authentically, you let go of *co-dependence*. You do not seek to have others dependent on you. You offer loving advice and then let go, confident of the outcome, whatever it is. How can you be confident of the outcome? By turning it over to Holy Spirit, the Universe, Guardian Angels or God, and by recognizing that you do not know what is best for others. When you live authentically, you let go of your own *dependence on the opinions of others*. You will hear their advice but not be dependent on their approval. You will welcome the loving advice of your friends, relatives, neighbors and others, and use your inner guidance to find your way.

BE COMPASSIONATE

The daily newspaper and the nightly news contain many examples of personal losses, physical injuries, deaths, and financial setbacks. Some of these strike us as unjust. We know of people losing their lives, loved ones, life savings, jobs, or health through no fault of their own or at the hands of someone. The child in us cries out, "It's not fair" and, in many cases, the event does violate our sense of fairness. We get angry sometimes, angry at the perpetrator, angry at the world in which this happens.

Think of letting go of your frustration around injustice. See the *injustice*, do what you can to eliminate it, and extend love to the people who are on the receiving end of the injustice, look for ways to relieve their physical and emotional pain, and forgive those responsible for the injustice. In addition, let go of your sense of injustice, regardless of how keenly you feel it. Instead, use the energy you have invested in your feelings to become motivated and to fuel your constructive responses.

. . . when you let it

The *daily news*—whether it is delivered by newspapers, TV, or radio—can have a significant impact on the way you think and feel. And it doesn't have to. You can let go of the news as a determinant of how you feel. You can be aware of it, recognize it is part of the play in which you are appearing each day, and choose not to get caught up in the drama. Much of the nightly news has a gossipy feel. It mostly consists of people reporting the activities of other people, with a lot of emphasis on what went wrong, or what might go wrong.

Much of the rest of the news seems to be speculation and opinions on what's happening, why it's happening, and what could happen next. The changes in prices of stocks and bonds reflect the opinions of the investor regarding what success individual businesses are going to have, what success groups of businesses (market sectors) are going to have, where our country's economy is going, and where the global economy is going. The people who are commenting on these prices and their changes are offering their opinions on these opinions.

What does this have to do with compassion? Behind the reports and the numbers are people doing their best to create prosperity for themselves, their families, their investors, their customers, and their suppliers. To let go of the daily financial news, reach behind the headlines and numbers and touch the people. Be compassionate towards them. Hold no resentment for what they did or didn't do. Let go of the drama of the financial world; notice that every time someone sells a share of stock or a bond, someone else buys it! The stock market is a place for working out various objectives and different opinions. Let go of the outcomes of your transactions and of those around you. If you have enough money to invest, feel the joy of it! Have no emotional investment in the outcomes, just feel the joy of it.

Power struggles and *competitiveness* exist between two or more individuals or groups who want the same thing when there is not enough to go around. First place prizes, presidencies (of companies or organizations), department heads, and admissions to prestigious schools are some examples. Losing a power struggle could give rise to resentment or jealousy. And winning a power struggle is unlikely to bring forth feelings of love and compassion for the others in the struggle. In being compassionate, you strive for both you and your associates to win (winwin); power struggles do not attract you.

Games can be different; the field, the court, the pool and other venues, are places where friends can compete strenuously and still be friends, appreciating each other and their efforts.

BE COOPERATIVE

St. Francis of Assisi has told us, "It is in giving that we receive." (See page 159.) Cooperation is a form of giving, that is, freely giving our time, energy, imagination, and talent to help others be who and what they wish. Don't cooperate for the rewards, the success, the recognition. When you help others and cooperate with them, you are more aware of yourself as a loving individual. That's the payoff. It's an inner experience that grows as you continue to be cooperative.

While I was in Japan, I learned that the Japanese people and society did things differently from *my way*, the American way. They used the same hand motion to say hello that we do to say good-bye. They lived in frame houses covered with paper. Their house numbers were assigned in the order in which the houses were built. It was polite (complimentary) to slurp tea noisily. I learned that my way was only my way and not *the* way. Although I have still not reached the point where I want to be, my experience in Japan has helped me to let go of having my way.

Look for opportunities to support the other person in having his or her way. As you do, you'll recognize it as a sign of cooperation, not weakness, and you can enjoy being supportive of others.

. . . when you let it

BE FORGIVING

If you are feeling *hurt* or *slighted,* you can find the source within yourself. No one is doing it to you. Your role is to forgive others who have apparently hurt or slighted you. Further, your role is to forgive the others *for what they have not done to you.* The beautiful logic behind this is that if no one is hurting you, you cannot forgive someone for the hurt he or she did not cause. So you simply forgive. What for? For you. The feelings of forgiveness are much more loving than the feelings of being hurt or slighted. And you can forgive yourself.

In my professional consulting practice for the improvement of chemical manufacturing, I have emphasized the value of creating a blame-free atmosphere. This is because blaming is an attack on the individual who is the object of the blame and will often engender a defensive reaction, a reaction born of fear. One of the precepts of W. Edwards Deming, the father of modern manufacturing improvements, is "Drive out fear," and a blame-free atmosphere does just that. Focusing on the problem and what needs to be done is much more effective—in both the short run and the long run—than finding someone to blame. This is equally true in all of our personal interactions. If you come to every situation from the vantage point of forgiveness, you will naturally be creating a blame-free atmosphere. Instead of making people fearful because they are wondering when they will be blamed, your forgiveness will foster loving kindness.

A negative *judgment* always precedes blaming someone. If, in the practice of forgiveness, you let go of judgment, you will have no cause for blame. This is not to suggest you must give up your distinctions between what works, or is effective, and what doesn't. In a blame-free work atmosphere, you retain your ability to discern what meets the requirements and customers' expectations and what doesn't. In a blame-free life, you keep your standards and expectations, and you notice when they are not met. In my home life, being on time has been a high priority for me and a much lower one for Sharon. We have often been late to church, concerts, etc. We have discussed being late, and we are now much more prompt than we used to be. I can't say I am free of blaming, but I did eventually let go of my emotional attachment to being on time. That in turn helped me to let go of my negative judgments. Forgiving her and being at ease if we were late seemed to be important in the process. She says my letting go also helped her be on time more often.

Without negative judgments, you would not feel *resentment*. The feeling of resentment is based on a false belief that someone has done something to you. Instead, assume "someone" is doing the best she or he can. So you have two ways to let go of resentment, both based on forgiveness: let go of negative judgments or see that no one is doing it to you, or both.

Getting even is a kind of revenge; "an eye for an eye and a tooth for a tooth" is the Old Testament version. For what? For what someone has done to you or to someone or something you care about. Has someone taken something belonging to you? Not kept an agreement with you? Shown you disrespect or attempted to discredit you? Abused you or your loved ones? These painful behaviors are not things anyone is doing to you. They are the actions of a person who is hurting, who doesn't feel good about himself or herself. The best you can do for them is reassure them, forgive them, and extend love to them.

This is not to imply we want to tolerate or condone abuse. As indicated in Chapter 6, in any abusive situation, moving to a place of physical and emotional safety is of paramount importance. When you are safe, you can begin to look upon the perpetrator with forgiveness and compassion.

BE LOVING

Jerry Jampolsky has written an introduction to *A Course in Miracles* entitled *Love is Letting Go of Fear.*[17] That idea is the theme here: as you let go of fear, love will grow and fill your life. You are a loving person, that is your true nature, and by letting go of every fearful thought, you will experience yourself that

. . . when you let it

way. Your progress may be a little slow at first, but you will move forward.

When we let go of longing, yearning and desire, we will simply be in touch with our true feelings; we will be loving. An old saying teaches us: "If you love someone, let her (or him) go. If she loves you, she will come back." And if she doesn't love you, she'll be a *lost love*. Then you can just love her and enjoy your loving feelings. If this is difficult, look at the co-dependence in your former relationship and consider letting it go.

In our everyday life, *resistance* is born of fear. When you are resisting, ask yourself, "What am I afraid of?" The answer may come easily: fear of being made wrong; of having to give up your self-image; of not having enough time, energy, or money; of losing control over some situation; or any other threatening situation. What are you to be afraid of? Nothing. Everything is okay just the way it is. Thinking of things to be afraid of may be the principal barrier to living unafraid.

As you accept the way life is and fearlessly live out of your acceptance, your resistance dissolves. How do you do that? One fearful thought at a time. Each time you are resisting, you can sense tight muscles in your neck, shoulders, abdomen, or legs or perhaps in more than one place at the same time. This is your opportunity to look at what is blocking you from being more loving; this is your time to forgive whoever or whatever is in the way of your doing so.

When you are resistant and fearful, reflect on this: you have been resistant and fearful before. In many cases, your fears were not realized, and looking back now you see nothing to have been afraid of. Remind yourself of these experiences. Extend love to the people you were afraid of; feel your love. Although some other situations may not have worked out the way you wanted, you lived through them, learned, and grew stronger. And, as you extend love to the people you once were afraid of, you will release the resistance holding you.

Aggression is never a part of being loving. Any use of force— verbal or physical—is contrary to being loving. Like resistance, aggression and *defensiveness* is rooted in fear. As with resistance, when you accept the way life is, you won't use force. The energy accompanying tendencies towards aggression is the same energy we use for our creativity. This is the foundation of win-win conflict resolution. The energy building up around a conflict is channeled into creative ways to resolve the conflict. This redirection of energy away from aggression and into creativity is an option always available to us. With practice, we can lovingly shift away from aggression and into creativity in every aspect of our lives.

When our *loved ones, relatives, friends, and co-workers have health issues,* we can love them and help them receive good care. A lot has been written on the role of the mind-body connection in healing, and we don't understand much of what goes on. We know of countless instances of spontaneous remission, miraculous healing, and renewal of bones. For example, at a simple level, I have had only two or three headaches in the last twenty years, apparently because I have consciously "chosen" not to have them. When I have felt a cold or a throat infection coming on, I have consciously "chosen" not to be sick. In so doing, I have had flashes of insight, remembering when I was "sick" as a child and feeling happy I didn't have to go to school. At age 60, I let go of my severe lifelong allergy to cats, and we now have three cats.

These experiences have shaken my belief in disease. As the son of a nurse, the nephew of three nurses, brother of a nurse, brother-in-law of a doctor and uncle of a doctor, I believed disease was "normal." I believed in terminal illnesses. I no longer hold steadfastly to these beliefs. I know of many people "beating the odds" and surviving. A friend of mine is one of the five percent to survive a particular form of cancer. Nevertheless, I don't avoid medical treatment—I have three stents and a pacemaker—and I extend love and encouragement to people who are having symptoms of any disease.

Many people have other challenges in their lives, perhaps relationships or finances. I choose not to respond to reports of these challenges with statements like, "Isn't that too bad?" "How awful!" "How could they (he, she)?" "You must feel awful!" and other expressions "buying into" what seems like a calamity to the person giving me the report. This is *getting caught up in the drama in the lives of your loved ones, relatives, friends, and co-workers.* Extending love is always appropriate. "What can I do to help?" "I want you to feel better" and "Take good care of yourself" are ways to express your love.

BE OKAY WITH YOURSELF

How does this differ from being authentic? Being okay with yourself means fully accepting who you are, "warts and all." Being authentic means looking past any imagined deficiencies and seeing yourself as you really are, whole, complete, and perfect.

A Course in Miracles states, " . . . I [you] need do nothing."9 If that's the case, you certainly don't need to *do more.* The people who depend on you need your love more than anything you can do for them. When you fully realize you don't need to do more, you might feel the kind of joy you feel on your vacations.

Do you think you are overweight or underweight for optimum health? If you do, you can choose to do something appropriate, or not. Regardless of your choice, you can still let go of your *weight as an issue,* something for you to worry about. And you can feel the joy of being fully alive.

We have already learned that if you need something, it will come to you. Living by this principle, you can know you're okay and you can let go of *acquisitiveness, financial issues* and *not having enough.*

You *let go of your health issues* when you see yourself as okay. You are not a victim. In a way that's analogous to the health issues of others, the best you can do for yourself is to love yourself and obtain good care, both from healthcare professionals and yourself. Work with your body, listen to it, give it the care it wants, and love it.

When you see you are okay and live by the principle *everything turns out right . . . when you let it,* you will have *no emotion-*

al investment in the outcome of anything. Anytime you feel emotional investment creeping into your consciousness, be reminded of the basic principle. This will help you feel the joy of living your life.

BE RELAXED

Some people have a need to *control* their surroundings including family, friends, and co-workers. If you are one of them, know that the need comes from being afraid, afraid of not being good enough, afraid that what's going on in your life will not turn out right. Being afraid is a chronic condition you can change. When you sense your muscles are tight, it is your clue to relax. Consciously relax all your muscles, not just the ones that grabbed your attention. When you are finished, relax them all again. Sometimes when you relax your shoulders, you will benefit by immediately doing it again, and then still again, each time lowering them a little more. Continue until further relaxation does not loosen the muscles any more. Or you might be living with more or less constant anxiety, and your tight muscles go unnoticed. After that, whenever you feel a surge of apprehension, relax your muscles the same way. (They will be tight even if you are unaware of them.) In any case, you don't have to exercise control over whatever worries you. See that *everything turns out right . . . when you let it.*

Letting go of schedules means letting go of the pressure of adhering to them while at the same time being reliable and on time. For the longest time, I resisted being on time for work (I often was late), for my flights, and for appointments. I was resisting the schedules in my life because I didn't want to give in to the authority that created them. I eventually got over that, partially because the success of my consulting business depended on my being prompt and partially because I worked with a man who was always late, sometimes very late, and I saw how disruptive that behavior was. To some extent, I allowed the pendulum to swing the other way and allowed myself to become

. . . when you let it

somewhat obsessive about being on time, but now I can be on time and relaxed. If we are always on time, we can be relaxed and feel the joy of living that way.

When people act in a way that doesn't conform with how you think they should, you might want to *figure it out*. Sometimes that can be a frustrating experience, as discussed in Chapter 5. So when people act in ways you don't understand, realize their behavior is not about you, it's about the other person. An effective response is to relax and extend love to the person who is calling for it.

BACK TO THE BEGINNING

As was suggested at the beginning of this chapter, the idea here is to choose a characteristic (attribute) you want to let go of. If you choose a new way of being, you will, perhaps slowly, let go of the unwanted characteristic. And as you let go of one characteristic, you can let go of another one more easily, and then another. And when you have a new way of being, forgiving perhaps, it will be easier for you to find another new way of being, such as loving or authentic. The new ways of being are not mutually exclusive, but more like threads in a tapestry you will weave.

A factor helping you in all this is "You are the person you would like to become." The new way of being will bring you closer to your true self. You are likely to encounter resistance in this process, and you can expect your resistance will diminish as you move forward. Other people in your life may resist the changes they see in you. If you are reassuring towards them, their resistance will diminish too.

Do you think this is difficult? Remember: "When faced with a difficult task, start." Take a small bite, a modest goal, and then realize the truth: "If at first you don't succeed, relax and you will." As you loosen your grip on the attribute you want to let go of, feel the joy of your new way of being.

everything turns out right . . .

SUMMARY

◈ When you let go, you feel joy.

◈ Be authentic: live out of your awareness of yourself as whole, complete, and perfect.

◈ Be compassionate; you can safely assume that everyone is doing the best they can.

◈ Be cooperative, knowing this: "It is in giving that we receive."

◈ Be forgiving; it is a gift to yourself.

◈ Be loving, without longing, without expectations, without conditions.

◈ Be okay with yourself: know that if you need something, it will come to you.

◈ Be relaxed: know that *everything turns out right . . . when you let it.*

◈ As you find a new way of being, it will become easier to find yet another.

Share your joy!

. . . when you let it

NOTES

1. Marcus Aurelius, *Meditations III*, page 10. Translation by Morris Hickey Morgan (1859-1910)

2. Alan Watts, *THIS IS IT*, First Vintage Book Edition, page 13 (1973)

3. *A Course in Miracles*, Foundation for Inner Peace, 13th printing (1984)

4. Neale Donald Walsch, *Conversations with God, Book 1*, Hampton Roads Publishing Company (1995)

5. *Scofield Study Bible, New International Version*, Oxford University Press Inc., Luke 6: 27—35 (1967)

6. W. Timothy Gallwey, *The Inner Game of Tennis*, Random House, Bantam Edition, page 7 (1974)

7. *Scofield Study Bible, New International Version*, Oxford University Press Inc., Matthew 14: 22-31 (1967)

8. Neale Donald Walsch, *Conversations with God, Book 1*, Hampton Roads Publishing Company, page 98 (1995)

9. *A Course in Miracles, Volume I: Text*, Foundation for Inner Peace, 13th printing, page 362 (1984)

10. Alan Watts, *THIS IS IT*, First Vintage Books Edition, page 24 (1973)

11. *Scofield Study Bible, New International Version*, Oxford University Press Inc., Matthew 18: 21-22 (1967)

12. A *Course in Miracles, Volume II: Workbook for Students*, Foundation for Inner Peace, 13th printing, page 8 (1984)

13. William Glasser, *Reality Therapy*, Harper & Row (1965)

14. Jampolsky, Gerald G., *Love Is Letting Go of Fear*, Bantam Books, pages 20-23 (1981)

15. Eknath Easwaran, *Meditation: Commonsense Directions for an Uncommon Life*, Nilgiri Press, pages 29-30 (1978)

everything turns out right . . .

16. Jill Jackson and Sy Miller, *The Peace Song*, Jan-Lee Music (1983)

17. Jampolsky, Gerald G., *Love Is Letting Go of Fear*, Bantam Books (1981)

. . . when you let it

Index

. . . when you let it

. . . when you let it

. . . when you let it

About the Author

Two decades ago, Charlie Ware was a successful chemical engineer and beloved mentor who fell into a life-changing experience that set him on a new spiritual path. Not long after, he discovered the guiding principle, *Everything turns out right . . . when you let it*, and called it *Charlie's Law*™.

Living his law and sharing it, Charlie has been a popular national speaker, leading numerous workshops in Conflict Resolution, *A Course in Miracles,* Creativity, and *Charlie's Law*™. Highly intelligent and down to earth, he is an original thinker and a funny, loving man whose audiences are profoundly transformed by his simple, universal wisdom.

Born and raised in the Bronx, Ware holds a BSE degree from Princeton University and MS and Ph.D. degrees from the University of Pennsylvania; he is a Fellow of the American Institute of Chemical Engineers. A consultant in the application of statistics to chemical manufacturing and an inventor, he is also the president of Charlie's Law™, Inc., a publisher of inspiring thoughts for every day.

OTHER PRODUCTS

Would you like reminders of Charlie's Law™ and its corollaries in your home or office, or to share these ideas with friends and family? We have several ways for you to put these ideas on the wall, on your refrigerator, or in the mail.

Posters

Beautiful, full color posters are available in two styles and two sizes, unframed or framed. *Everything turns out right . . . when you let it* appears on each poster, along with the other chapter titles in *Murphy's Law Repealed!*

Greeting Cards

Twelve greeting cards are available, individually or in boxed sets. A different color photograph appears on the front of each 5" x 7" card, along with the first part of one of the Charlie's Law™ corollaries. The rest of the corollary and *Everything turns out right . . . when you let it* are printed on the inside.

Magnets

Our magnets are 2½ inches square, with glass on the front and a copper-finished edge. Charlie's Law™ and three corollaries are individually printed over different water-color scenes. Buy one, or the entire set of four.

For more information or to order:

Call 1-877-723-1070 toll-free, or call 727-723-1070.
Or write to us at: Charlie's Law, Inc.,

P.O. Box 807
Safety Harbor, FL 34695-0807

Or visit our website: **www.CharliesLawInc.com**, where you can view and order any of these products.

ORDER FORM

Secure Online Ordering: www.MurphysLawRepealed.com

Telephone Orders: 727-723-1070 or toll-free 877-723-1070
Please have your credit card ready.

Fax Orders: 727-723-8169. Send this completed order form.

Mail Orders: Charlie's Law, Inc.
P.O. Box 807, Safety Harbor, FL, 34695-0807

PLEASE SEND: AMOUNT:

____ copies of *Murphy's Law Repealed!* @ $14.95 ea.   _____

FL residents please include state/local sales tax   _____

$3.00 shipping for the first book   _____
(media rate, call for rates if faster shipping desired)

$2.00 for each additional book   _____

TOTAL   _____

Name: _____

Address: _____

City: _____ State: _____ Zip: _____

Daytime phone: _____

E-mail address: _____

Payment: ___Check ___Credit Card

___American Express ___MasterCard   ___VISA

Card number: _____

Name on card: _____ Exp. Date: _____

"These dynamic principles should be posted on every office wall."
—Alan Cohen, author of *Why Your Life Sucks and What
You Can Do About It* and *I Had It All the Time*

___ I want to be reminding myself of Charlie's Law™ and its principles. Please send me **free** information on:

___ Posters ___ Greeting cards ___ Magnets